# Work Smarter with Speed Reading

*To Morris Taylor*

# Work Smarter with Speed Reading

Tina Konstant

For UK order enquiries: please contact Bookpoint Ltd, 130 Milton Park, Abingdon, Oxon OX14 4SB. Telephone: +44 (0) 1235 827720. Fax: +44 (0) 1235 400454. Lines are open 09.00–17.00, Monday to Saturday, with a 24-hour message answering service. Details about our titles and how to order are available at www.teachyourself.com

For USA order enquiries: please contact McGraw-Hill Customer Services, PO Box 545, Blacklick, OH 43004-0545, USA. Telephone: 1-800-722-4726. Fax: 1-614-755-5645.

For Canada order enquiries: please contact McGraw-Hill Ryerson Ltd, 300 Water St, Whitby, Ontario L1N 9B6, Canada. Telephone: 905 430 5000. Fax: 905 430 5020.

Long renowned as the authoritative source for self-guided learning – with more than 50 million copies sold worldwide – the **Teach Yourself** series includes over 500 titles in the fields of languages, crafts, hobbies, business, computing and education.

*British Library Cataloguing in Publication Data*: a catalogue record for this title is available from the British Library.

*Library of Congress Catalog Card Number*: on file. 44279460    8/10

First published in UK 2010 by Hodder Education, part of Hachette UK, 338 Euston Road, London NW1 3BH.

First published in US 2010 by The McGraw-Hill Companies, Inc.

This edition published 2010.

Previously published as *Teach Yourself Speed Reading*.

The **Teach Yourself** name is a registered trade mark of Hodder Headline.

Copyright © 2010 Tina Konstant

Typeset by MPS Limited, A Macmillan Company.

Printed in Great Britain for Hodder Education, an Hachette UK Company, 338 Euston Road, London NW1 3BH, by CPI Cox & Wyman, Reading, Berkshire RG1 8EX.

The publisher has used its best endeavours to ensure that the URLs for external websites referred to in this book are correct and active at the time of going to press. However, the publisher and the author have no responsibility for the websites and can make no guarantee that a site will remain live or that the content will remain relevant, decent or appropriate.

Hachette UK's policy is to use papers that are natural, renewable and recyclable products and made from wood grown in sustainable forests. The logging and manufacturing processes are expected to conform to the environmental regulations of the country of origin.

Impression number     10 9 8 7 6 5 4 3 2 1

Year                  2014 2013 2012 2011 2010

**Front cover:** Comstock Images/Getty Images

**Back cover:** © Jakub Semeniuk/iStockphoto.com, © Royalty-Free/Corbis, © agencyby/iStockphoto.com, © Andy Cook/iStockphoto.com, © Christopher Ewing/iStockphoto.com, © zebicho – Fotolia.com, © Geoffrey Holman/iStockphoto.com, © Photodisc/Getty Images, © James C. Pruitt/iStockphoto.com, © Mohamed Saber – Fotolia.com

# Contents

# Meet the author

**When I first wrote this book, I thought almost entirely in terms of 'speed reading': reading faster, getting through more information more quickly, understanding, remembering and using information you get from books.**

Now that a few years have passed and I've moved from tertiary education and into the glorious world of work, bills, mortgages and a desperate need for sun-seeking winter holidays, I need to absorb a different type of information from a multitude of sources and apply it to more than passing exams or submitting essays.

Speed reading is not just about reading fast, it's about managing information. That's what this book is all about.

I hope you enjoy the new edition.

Tina Konstant

# *Only got a minute?*

The main reason most of us read at an average rate of 150–300 words per minute is because that is approximately the rate at which we speak.

While you are reading this paragraph, listen to what is going on inside your head. Do you hear a voice inside your head while you are reading? Are you 'saying' the words in your mind while you read? This is happening because of the way you were taught to read.

When you were taught to read, you learned to recognize one letter or sound at a time, then, when you mastered that, you moved on to recognizing one word at a time. The next step was being able to read out loud so that your teacher could see that you had learned to recognize the words accurately. Then you were left to read 'to yourself'. That 'inner voice' became a habit. Instead of reading out loud you read silently. You learned that you had to hear the words to understand what you were reading rather than see them.

So when we talk about reading with your ears instead of your eyes – that is exactly what is happening: you are reading/speaking 'to yourself' at the same rate as when you read/speak out loud.

When you first learned to read, reading 'to yourself' was slow because you were still learning to recognize the words. As you read more and got further into the education system your reading rate increased because your vocabulary increased. But your reading strategy did not change.

To increase your 'word-per-minute' reading rate you must first accelerate, only then can you eliminate the sound in your head (often referred to as sub-vocalization).

Two methods for achieving this are:

## Method 1: Using a guide

Place a guide (pen, pencil or finger) underneath the first or second word of a line. Move the guide smoothly across the page from the beginning to the end of each line. Repeat on each line. Move the guide a little faster than is comfortable. Make the movement smooth and swift.

If the guide pauses, then it is likely to be following (instead of leading) your eye. You will continue to sub-vocalize and your speed will not increase. When the guide moves fast and smoothly, your eyes are forced to follow and your reading rate will increase. The faster you move your guide, the less you will sub-vocalize because your inner voice will be unable to keep up. This technique eliminates the habit of reading one word at a time, and stops your attention jumping around the page unnecessarily.

**Important note!!**

Speed reading is a skill. Developing that skill does not mean you have to read fast all the time. The technical content of the material, print size, your mood, familiarity with the subject and your purpose, are some of the factors that will affect the speed at which you read. The ability to read quickly allows you to choose how fast or slow you read.

# Method 2: Mostly reading

This technique is good for subject matter with which you are familiar, but you want to make sure that you miss nothing out.

Read the first sentence of the paragraph. Skim the rest of the paragraph for key words and, if necessary, read the last sentence of the paragraph.

# 5 Only got five minutes?

Reading fast is great – but do you remember and apply what you read and learn? The purpose of this book is to provide you with the skills you need to extract and *use* relevant information from the mass available to you.

---

## Top three most frequently asked questions:

**What is the fastest possible reading speed?**

If there is a limit on the speed at which people can read, we don't know what that is. We do know that some people can read a book the size of *War and Peace* in less than 20 minutes and retain and recall enough to answer questions at least as well as those who read 'normally'!

**How do I remember what I read – when I need to remember it?**

The ability to retain and recall is the most relevant outcome. If you do not plan to remember what you read, why read it in the first place?

**Is speed reading easy to learn?**

Speed reading is easy to learn, and you can learn it quickly. Only one part of the Five-Step System presented in this book requires practice. The rest works just because you use it.

By the time you have used the five-step system you will have:

▶ *explored the material at least three times*
▶ *read what you need to have read*
▶ *found the information you require*

- *integrated new information with what you already know*
- *have accurate recall of the information*

Moreover, you will have done it quickly without missing material important to your purpose.

---

## The five-step system

### Step 1: Prepare

This step should take no more than a few minutes no matter how big the book is.

Lack of focus interferes with concentration. It makes reading frustrating. The preparation stage will give you the focus you need to get what you want out of the material as quickly as possible.

To prepare (and establish your purpose), ask yourself three questions:

- *What do you already know about the subject you are reading?*
- *What do you need to know (general information or the answer to a specific question)?*
- *How do you intend to use the new information (write an essay, exam, report, general interest, give a presentation) and when (next week, next month, next year, right now...)*

### Step 2: Structure

For a 200-page book, studying the structure of the book or document should take between one and ten minutes, depending on the length of the book and your purpose.

**During Step 2:**

▶ *Read the front and back covers, inside flaps, table of contents, index, and scan the bibliography.*
▶ *Determine the structure of the book; chapter headings, sub-headings, pictures, graphs, cartoons and images.*
▶ *Strike out parts of the book that you are sure you don't need.*
▶ *Highlight areas you think you do need.*
▶ *Re-affirm your decision about what you want from the book.*

If it becomes clear that the book does not contain what you need, put it away. You will have saved yourself hours of work.

## Step 3: Language

The purpose of step three is to familiarize yourself with the language in the book. Is it full of jargon? Is the language complicated? Are there any acronyms?

Becoming familiar with the language of a 200-page book should take about five to ten minutes.

▶ *Scan the pages at about a page every two seconds.*
▶ *Look for words that stand out and highlight them: names; long or technical words; bold or italics words linked to your purpose.*
▶ *Study the language: Is it technical, non-technical, user-friendly? Are you familiar with it?*
▶ *Do you need to refer to a dictionary?*
▶ *Note the meaning of acronyms as you read.*

Your familiarity with the language determines the speed at which you will be able to read. During this step you might also recognize recurring themes and concepts. Highlight anything relevant to your purpose.

### Step 4: Content

Most well-written material outlines the main element of the chapter in the first paragraph with the main idea of each paragraph in its first sentence. For more detail read:

▶ *the first paragraph of every section*
▶ *the first sentence of every paragraph (and, if the paragraph is long, the last).*

The more thoroughly you highlight, underline, circle, take notes and mind-map what you read, the easier Step 5 will be.

### Step 5: Selective reading

You will now be in a position to select 'intelligently' what you need or want to read.

**Insight**

You will probably have read this section in less than five minutes. If you haven't read the one-minute summary, go back and do that now. These two summaries together will help you read the ten-minute summary (and the rest of the book) in a fraction of the time.

# 10 Only got ten minutes?

## Remember what you read

**No matter how fast you read, unless you remember what you read you will have wasted your time.**

The TOP THREE methods for remembering what you read are:

1 **Use new information.** *Explain it to someone, discuss it, write it, construct arguments for and against it, think about it and apply it.*
2 **Have a purpose.** *Always know why you are reading something and when you are going to use it.*
3 **Use the Five-Step Reading System.** *This system allows you to select exactly what you need to read therefore avoiding any unnecessary and distracting material that hinders concentration and recall.*

## Other memory techniques

### LINEAR

Make notes as you read or after each section. Include your own thoughts, ideas and cross-references. The more you include your own ideas the stronger and more reliable your long-term memory will be.

### KEY WORDS

Highlight words that carry the message. If you make notes separately, ensure that key words are correct. This avoids creating a list of words that makes no sense when you review at a later date.

### MARGIN READING

A book is a form of communication from one person to another. Take ownership of a book by adding your thoughts to the author's. Underline, circle, highlight essential areas and note whether you agree or disagree. Make note of your reasoning. Mark what you do or don't understand. You should only do this if the book belongs to you. If not, use Post-it notes. All of this will make reviewing easier and more meaningful.

### MIND-MAPPING

- ▶ *Place the key idea in the centre of a horizontal page.*
- ▶ *Main ideas form thick branches from the centre.*
- ▶ *Secondary ideas flow from the main ideas.*
- ▶ *Tertiary ideas flow from secondary ideas. And so on until you reach the finest detail.*
- ▶ *Use colour and symbols.*
- ▶ *One word or idea per line.*

---

## Improving speed and memory

This quick exercise will help improve your memory and increase your speed.

Using a guide, read one page as fast as you can. Stop and summarize what you remember. Read five to ten pages like this every day, gradually increasing the number of pages before you stop to recall what you read. Start with a familiar subject. As your ability, confidence and comfort increase, take on more challenging material.

### STRETCH YOUR SPEED: THE 'ONE-MINUTE TRIP'

- ▶ *Read for one minute, then count how many lines you have read.*
- ▶ *Continue reading for another minute, this time, reading two lines more than last time.*

- *Then read four more, then six more, then eight, then ten and so on.*
- *Always read for good comprehension and recall. As soon as you feel you are not understanding or remembering the text, stay at that level until you become a little more confident before gradually increasing speed again.*
- *Reading quickly requires concentration. If you don't understand what you read, then you will not easily remember it and your concentration will fade. If this happens you will become bored and disappointed.*
- *With practice, your concentration will improve. As it does, stretch the 'one-minute trip' to two minutes, then to four and six and eight … and so on.*

## METRONOME PACING

Invest in a small, cheap electronic metronome at any music store. Practise this for two minutes then relax for five:

- *Set the metronome at its slowest speed, and read one line per 'tick'.*
- *Every half page or so, increase the pace of the metronome by one beat per minute until you reach the fastest speed.*
- *Then, relax.*
- *The metronome will reach a speed at which you will not be able to read every word. This exercise 'pushes' your eye and brain to see and absorb more than one word at a time without sub-vocalization. This gradually stretches your ability. When you reach a rate at which you feel you cannot take in what you read, maintain that speed. Make sure that even though you may not take in the content, you see and recognize (but not say) every word. For instance, if there is a foreign word in the text, you would recognize it.*
- *Imagine driving down a motorway at 85 miles per hour. As you approach a town you reduce your speed to 30. You might think you are travelling at 30 until the police stop you and inform you that you were travelling at 40 or 50 – much faster than you thought.*

The similarity between driving and speed reading doesn't stop there. Travelling at 70 miles per hour you have to concentrate and don't have time to look at the scenery. When speed reading you are reading so fast that your mind can't wander as much as it can at '30 miles per hour'. You are more focused.

## Treat your eyes: preventing and curing eyestrain

Your eyes need rest. The more relaxed they are the longer you will be able to read. Here are a few simple things you can do to prevent and cure eyestrain:

▶ *Palming is an excellent eye-relaxing exercise. Rub your hands together until they are warm. Then close your eyes and cover them with your hands so that no light gets in. Do not press against your eyeballs: if you were to do so you could damage them. Cover your eyes like this for as long as you have time to.*
▶ *Many people who have eye problems compound them by not blinking. If you do not blink your eyes will become dry. While reading (especially from a PC monitor) be aware of your eyes, blink often and water them. If it helps, put a sign above your PC to remind yourself to blink.*
▶ *If your eyes feel particularly tired there are a number of very good eyewashes you can get from any pharmacy. Follow the instructions carefully when you use them and if necessary check with your optician or your doctor. If you wear contact lenses it is even more important to take care of your eyes while you are reading.*
▶ *When you read, your eyes are limited to how much they move. An excellent way to relieve stress is to practise eye exercises. First, look straight ahead, then look up as far as you can, down as far as you can, then to the left, then to the right. Then, look to the top left, top right, bottom right and bottom left. Hold each gaze for only a couple of seconds. Then squeeze your eyes shut and repeat the exercise. When you have finished the exercise, palm for a few minutes.*

## READING FROM A PC MONITOR WITHOUT STRAINING YOUR EYES

- ▶ **Font size and type.** *If someone has sent you a document and the font is difficult to read, either due to its size or type, change it. Serif fonts are easier and quicker to read.*
- ▶ **Screen contrast.** *Make sure the background contrasts the text on the screen. Keep your screen clear and clutter free.*
- ▶ **Screen interference.** *Have as little around your screen as possible. Sometimes it is tempting to have all the icons on display. The more you have around your screen the smaller the screen space. Only have what is necessary for the work you are doing.*
- ▶ **Screen savers.** *There are screen savers on the market now that remain active all the time. The one that held my attention for quite some time was a sheep that ran around my screen while I worked. Not only does it help to relax your eyes and prevents you from staring at the screen but a sheep chasing frogs across the screen is good for your sense of humour. Anything humorous is good for your stress level, which in turn is good for concentration. It is important, however, to maintain the balance between humour and distraction.*
- ▶ **Screen position.** *Keep the screen a comfortable distance away from you. It should be at least arm's length away. Also, avoid having the screen directly in front of a window. The contrast in light can be uncomfortable and the activity outside can be distracting.*
- ▶ **Comfort.** *Working at a PC means that the only parts of your body that get any exercise are your fingers. Stop, stretch your body and do the eye exercises every 20 to 30 minutes.*

---

## Distractions and solutions

Distractions can prevent effective reading and accurate recall.

### CONCENTRATION

- ▶ *Take breaks often (approximately five minutes every 30 minutes) to ensure peak concentration.*

- *Have a purpose.*
- *Use a guide, especially if you are feeling tired or if the material is challenging.*
- *Take notes as you read.*

### COMFORT

Ensure you have fresh air and adequate light. Make yourself as comfortable as possible without feeling sleepy.

### MENTAL DISTRACTION

The expert at distracting you is you! When your mind wanders you have often not decided to spend the time on a particular task. So, before you begin to read, commit to a certain amount of time and do it. Realize that you are in control.

### LIGHT

Daylight is best. If there is none, then there should not be too much contrast between the light under which you are working and the rest of the room. This helps prevent eyestrain. The main source of light should come over the shoulder opposite your writing hand.

### VOCABULARY

Underline unfamiliar words. Look up the words at the end of the paragraph, page, section or as appropriate. This improves your comprehension and your vocabulary. The better your vocabulary, the faster your reading will be.

If you want more details, please read the rest of the book! But do yourself a favour and use the Five-Step System (see Chapter 1). You'll get through it in a fraction of the time!

# Introduction

Brief outline of each chapter

### CHAPTER 1: THE FIVE-STEP READING SYSTEM

This chapter covers one of the core techniques of the book. Reading it will give you the skills that will help you:

▶ *empty your in-tray quickly*
▶ *sort through piles of paperwork that have built up over the years*
▶ *read books that you've been wanting to read for years*
▶ *get through your reading at work in a quarter of the time it currently takes you*

### CHAPTER 2: SPEED READING

In this chapter you will learn how to take a flexible approach to your reading, how to find information fast and how to extract the message from the document without wasting time.

### CHAPTER 3: IT'S ALL IN THE WORDS – DEVELOPING YOUR VOCABULARY

The better your vocabulary is, the faster you will be able to read. This chapter is especially useful if you are reading a second language or if the material you are covering is technical or specialized.

### CHAPTER 4: CONCENTRATION

Without concentration there will be no memory. This is a practical chapter with exercises to help you increase your concentration, wherever you have to work.

## CHAPTER 5: MEMORY

If you do not remember what you read, you may as well not begin reading. This chapter will give you an insight into how your memory works and what may be happening when it does not. A selection of approaches to remembering what you are reading is included in this chapter. Look at them all and choose those which you could use for the different types of reading you do.

## CHAPTER 6: A BOOK IS A BOOK IS A BOOK

Or is it?

Every type of reading should be approached differently. In this chapter you will find different strategies that will make reading a newspaper in ten minutes a cinch and reading for work a doddle.

## CHAPTER 7: YOUR EYES AND EFFECTIVE READING

Your eyes are your most important reading tool. The chapter will help you take care of your eyes, prevent eyestrain and improve your reading rate by increasing what you can perceive within your visual span. This chapter has exercises and practical ideas to make your eyes work better for you.

## CHAPTER 8: DISTRACTIONS AND SOLUTIONS

Wherever you are, whatever you are doing, there will be something to distract you. This chapter links closely with Chapter 4 (Concentration) and Chapter 5 (Memory). The fewer the distractions, the faster and more productive your reading will be. Solutions to a number of different distractions are described.

## CHAPTER 9: REAL-WORLD READING

Most reading is done under pressure – in one way or another, time is the critical factor. If people ever give you documents to read and then stand waiting while you finish them, this is the chapter to read. It will also help you prioritize your reading and prevent yourself from becoming an information bottleneck.

## CHAPTER 10: WORKING AND STUDYING FOR A LIVING

If you do any kind of studying and also have a full-time job or look after a family you will find this chapter very useful. In it you will find ways to simplify and organize your reading and reduce the risk of panicking a week before an exam. If, however, you have only a week to go until the exam there is a strategy in this chapter that will help you make the best use of that time.

## CHAPTER 11: USEFUL INFORMATION AND SPEED PRACTICE TEST

This is a support and reference chapter with additional information that will help you increase your vocabulary and make reading easier. You may want to record in a notebook any extra information you come across that helps you extend your vocabulary.

## CHAPTER 12: WHAT NEXT?

How will you apply what you have learned? This chapter will help you design a 21-day programme that will assist you in integrating what you have learned into your day-to-day activities. Also, there are ideas on how to teach someone else.

# 1

........................................................................................

# The five-step reading system

In this chapter you will learn:
- **about the five steps: prepare, preview, passive, active, selective**
- **how to read for levels of meaning**
- **about reading with a purpose**

_____

## Introduction to the five-step system

By the time you complete the five steps in the system you will have:

▶ *Explored the material at least three times.*
▶ *Read what you need to have read.*
▶ *Integrated the new knowledge into what you already know.*
▶ *Gained an accurate recall of the information.*
▶ *Found the information you require.*

Most importantly, you will have spent a fraction of the time you might otherwise have spent learning these skills.

To avoid slipping back into old reading habits, closely follow the five-step system outlined in this book. Once you are familiar with it you can adapt it to any type of reading – articles, newspapers, memos, books, magazines and so on – by combining and omitting steps.

The five-step system has one over-riding rule: Always know why you are reading something.

> **Insight**
>
> If you glanced over the last sentence, it doesn't matter because by the end of this book I'll have said it again: The one over-riding rule of the five-step system is: know your purpose! It doesn't matter what your reason is for reading something – as long as you have a reason.

The five steps in the system are as follows:

1 *Prepare.*
2 *Preview.*
3 *Passive reading.*
4 *Active reading.*
5 *Selective reading.*

This system is based on a process that simply asks you to *highlight* and *eliminate*. As you use the system, your aim is to highlight areas for further study and eliminate those that you are certain you do not need.

Depending on how much you want from the book, Steps 1 to 4 could take between 5 and 40 minutes for a book of 300 pages. The time that you spend on Step 5 will depend on how much detailed information you want from the material.

Steps 1 to 5 will now be outlined. Read through this section once, then using a non-fiction book on a subject you are interested in try the system out. For the moment, forget about trying to read fast. We'll get to that later.

## Step 1: Prepare

One of the reasons why reading can be frustrating is a lack of concentration. This has as much to do with your thoughts as your surroundings. One of the serious distractions is tension. When you are approaching a large volume of reading, especially if the subject is new to you, tension may rise. One way to diminish initial tension is to establish that you already know something about the subject. Another, to use if you know that you do not know very much, is to formulate questions that will help you improve your knowledge and achieve your objective.

The main purpose of the preparation step is to build the framework (made up of questions and answers) onto which you will fit everything you learn as you read.

## Insight

Take a minute to think about what you are about to read and notice what questions your curiosity demands answers to. The more questions you ask, the more interested you'll be in the material. Develop the discipline of doing this even if what you are reading is a little dull.

Questions are important; without them you will find no answers. For every piece of information you place on your framework ask questions – who, what, where, when, why, how. There is no such thing as a silly question. Questions that are labelled as such are generally the ones that are difficult to answer. Think back to when you were a child and you asked a perfectly good question. If your parents could not, or did not want to, answer it, did they say, 'Don't ask such silly questions', leaving you feeling bewildered and ignorant? Always ask questions. It is better not to find the answer than never to ask the question. The more you know and the more questions you ask, the more you will be able to make sense of the subject.

The preparation stage helps you focus on the task:

▶ **Write down** *what you already know about the subject; key words are sufficient.*
▶ **Decide** *what you want from the book: is it general information, enough to write a report on or simply the answer to a specific question?*

> ▶ *Always* **ask** *yourself these three questions:*
>    **1** *Why am I reading this in the first place?*
>    **2** *What do I already know?*
>    **3** *What do I need to know?*

In other words... what is your purpose?

Getting yourself into a learning state is important.
This will help maximum concentration. Chapter 4, which deals with concentration, provides a number of methods that will help you focus on what you have to do, whether you are surrounded by distractions at home or in the midst of mayhem at the office.

## Insight

This step is essential. Even if you only take 30 seconds to prepare it will put you in the right frame of mind to concentrate on what you you're reading. Whether it's your mail or the *Encyclopaedia Britannica*, take time to prepare. Don't miss out the first step.

## Step 2: Preview

The purpose of previewing a book is to become familiar with its structure:

- ▶ *What does it look like?*
- ▶ *Are there summaries or conclusions?*
- ▶ *Is it all text?*
- ▶ *Are there any pictures?*
- ▶ *What size is the print?*
- ▶ *Does the font selected make it easy to read?*
- ▶ *Is the text broken up into sections?*
- ▶ *Is it a series of paragraphs?*

For a 300-page book, the overview should take about 10 minutes.

- ▶ **Read** *the front and back covers, the inside flaps, and the table of contents and have a look at the index, glossary and bibliography.*
- ▶ **Determine** *the structure of the book: chapter headings, sub-headings, pictures, graphs, cartoons and images.*
- ▶ **Eliminate** *the parts of the book that you are sure you don't need.*
- ▶ **Highlight** *areas you think you do need.*
- ▶ **Re-affirm** *your decision about what you want from the book.*
- ▶ *If it becomes clear that the book does not contain what you need, put it away. You will have saved yourself hours of work.*

There is a vast amount of information you can glean from each of the stages of your preview. Here are some ideas about what you should be looking for during this stage:

### THE COVER

The cover is the first call for a book. Any picture on the front is designed to attract your attention; it is therefore important to look beyond the picture to find out whether the book will be useful to you.

### Back-page blurb

This should give a good indication of what the book contains. It often contains promises, such as: 'If you read this book you will get …'. You may also be able to gauge the book's readability; if the back-page blurb is written in complex language, the rest of the book may be the same. If on the other hand it is clear, straightforward and easy to understand, there is a better chance of the book being easy reading.

### Inside flaps

Most hard-back books and even some soft-backs have information on the inside of the covers. This usually consists of summaries, biographical information and a photograph of the author. Reading this will give you information about the author and what point of view they might be taking.

## FOREWORD

The foreword, hardly ever read, is probably the most important section to cover at the preview stage. Another expert in the field usually writes it. It will almost always contain information about the author and their experience in the field they are writing in.

## TABLE OF CONTENTS

The contents table is intended to help you find your way through a book and is likely to be the section to which you refer most often. When you make a first pass at the table of contents, make notes as you go. If you know that you do not need the contents of a chapter, make a note about why you think you do not need it. For the chapters that you do want, note what it is you expect to find or questions you want answers to.

## GRAPHICS, PICTURES AND CARTOONS

These may be excellent sources of information. They contain information about the topic in a pictorial format. Since most of us remember pictures better than words, they will help you remember what you are reading. Do not just glance at graphs and pictures; study them, read the titles and any explanations provided and work out how they will fit into the framework you began to build in Step 1.

## TABLES

These are useful but can sometimes be confusing without background knowledge about what they contain. Look briefly at the tables without attempting to memorize or fully understand what they contain. If a brief explanation is attached to the table then read that, but without spending much time on it. The information will become clearer at Step 4 – Active reading.

### INDEX

Next to the table of contents, this is the most valuable section in the book. The index will give you detailed information in a different format from the contents table:

▶ *If you are looking for information on a specific aspect of the subject or an answer to a specific question you may find a reference to it without further reading.*
▶ *The index will give you a very clear indication of the detail the book has on your subject.*

### GLOSSARY

This section is useful to skim during this step and you will certainly find it most useful in Step 3 – Passive reading, when you are studying the language of the text. While you are reading the sections you have selected the glossary will be invaluable – place a marker at the start of the section so that when you need to determine the meaning of a word you will be able to find it quickly. If you are studying from the book, check whether you may photocopy the glossary so that you can add notes to it easily as you work.

### BIBLIOGRAPHY

The bibliography may indicate some of the books the author used as reference during the development of the book. It will also give an idea of what level the book is pitched at. If the books listed in the bibliography are all familiar to you, the book may not be sufficiently advanced for your needs. If they are new to you then it will be a good guide for further study.

On the basis of the information gathered during this step, you will be able to think more clearly about what the text covers. At this stage, review your purpose. Is it still the same as you stated before you previewed the book or has it changed because of what you have learnt?

At this stage you should also begin to be able to stretch your knowledge and understanding of what the author is trying to say. If, however, the author's point is still not clear, try to decide what assumptions the author is making.

All too often, specialists will write on their particular subject forgetting that many of the people who will be reading it will not have had the years of training, research and exposure to the subject that they have had. As a consequence, the language may be complex and basic explanations may be lacking. If this is the case, consider what questions you might need to answer before you can continue with the text. With those questions in mind, carry on to Step 3.

**Insight**

In Steps 2, 3 and 4 it will be tempting to read just a little more than is required for that step. Don't give in! See how much you can get through as quickly as possible, then select what you really want to read and take your time on that.

## Step 3: Passive reading

Now that you are prepared and know the structure of the book, this step will familiarize you with the **language** and the **organization** of the book. Is it full of jargon? Is the author a 'linguafan'? How is the information organized? Are there a lot of examples? Does the book take you through a step-by-step process?

Knowing how a book is organized will help you to identify key ideas and sentences in Step 4 – Active reading. The information may be arranged in a number of ways:

▸ **Chronological** – *First, second, third or by date.*
▸ **Examples** – *If there seem to be stories in the text, then perhaps*

*the stories are the evidence for arguments that the author states elsewhere.*

▶ **Advantages and disadvantages** – *To uncover this structure look for words like 'but', 'on the other hand' and 'however'.*

▶ **Process** – *Activity A leads to activity B and on to activity C.*

▶ **Most important/least important**– *Does the author place the core of the information at the start or at the end? Most newspaper stories will have the most important information at the start of the story, followed by the detail necessary to say more about the actual incident and perhaps finally comment from those involved or the opinion of the journalist.*

The passive reading step works best if you thoroughly completed Step 1 – Prepare.

It should take only between 10 and 15 minutes to read a 300-page book passively:

▶ **Scan** *the pages at a rate of about a page every one to two seconds.*

▶ **Highlight** *words that stand out. They may be names, long or technical words or words in* **bold** *or* italic.

▶ *Decide if the* **language** *is technical, non-technical or user-friendly. Are you familiar with it?*

▶ *Look out for words that will give you a* **clue** *to how the information is structured. Start looking for key ideas.*

▶ *Make a note of where the* **key arguments** *seem to be.*

## Insight

Know your purpose! If you don't, then Step 3 will be a waste of your time because you won't know what you are looking for. Experiment: Look around and notice everything red. Now, close your eyes and recall everything blue. What did you notice? You see what you look for.

## Step 4: Active reading

The main purpose of active reading is to identify the main ideas of a text. There are *two* reasons why this may be a challenge:

▶ *You might not know enough about the text or the author to recognize what the ideas or arguments are. This is like being asked whether you have any questions about a subject you know nothing about – you do not know enough to know what questions to ask. The more thoroughly you carry out Steps 1 to 3 and the clearer your purpose is, the easier it will be to find main ideas.*

▶ *The second challenge is that you may not know where in the text the main ideas are likely to be explained. Although the main idea of most well-written material is in the first sentence of the paragraph, it may be in the middle or at the end instead.*

### FINDING THE MAIN IDEA

Knowing the type of material you are reading will help you determine where the main idea is likely to be. A text written to inform will probably have the key sentence at the start of the paragraph. If the purpose is to entertain then the key information will more than likely be at the end (like the punch-line in a joke). If the text is there to persuade you, you may find key information at the start or in the middle. During Steps 1 and 3 look for the location of key information; this will help you to determine the nature of the text.

### FOR MORE DETAIL

This is the first time you will be doing anything resembling reading:

▶ *Determine the type of material you are reading.*
▶ *Read the* **first paragraph of every chapter** *and* **the first and last** (if the paragraph is long) **sentence of every paragraph.**

▶ *As you progress through the text, begin to identify where the main idea is likely to be and focus more attention on those sections.*

▶ *Avoid reading entire paragraphs. This will slow you down.*

The key question to ask during this step is:

▶ *What point is the author trying to make?*

Cross out, highlight, underline, circle and take notes as you read. Later in this book you will learn how to mind-map (see pp. 80–81). The more thoroughly you do this, the easier selecting what you really need to read will be.

## ANALYSE YOUR READING

Before you launch into Step 5 (Selective reading), take a little time to think about what you have read so far:

▶ *Did you have any difficulty with the context, vocabulary or content of the book?*
▶ *Did the material you read evoke any thoughts or feelings that were out of the ordinary?*
▶ *What was your attitude before you started reading? Has it changed now?*
▶ *As you went through Steps 1 to 4 did you become less interested in the material or more interested?*
▶ *How much time did you spend? Could you have reduced it?*
▶ *Did you get drawn into any particular section?*
▶ *Did you find what you were looking for?*
▶ *Are your notes clear?*

The third question, on attitude, is very important. If you feel negative about the task, your motivation and concentration will diminish and selecting what you need to read accurately may be more difficult to accomplish.

## Step 5: Selective reading

### Thought experiment (don't actually do this unless you want to waste a great deal of time and petrol!)

Imagine you are to take a trip from London to Edinburgh. You will use country roads as far as possible. Imagine you have never taken such a trip before, but still you decide not to take a map. On your arrival in Edinburgh, check your time, including the time taken by detours and by asking directions. Make the trip a second time using a map, and then compare the difference in time between the two journeys.

The same applies to reading. The first four steps, from preparation to active reading, create a map for you to follow. When you know where you are going and how you are going to get there, the task is much easier to accomplish.

The purpose of the first four steps is to allow you to select what you need or want to read and help you read it **intelligently**.

During the first four steps you have decided what it is you want to read, what answers you are looking for and what your interest in the subject is. You have studied the structure of the book, you are familiar with its language, you have read some of the content, giving you an excellent understanding of what the book contains. You can now select the sections you really need to read without worrying about whether you have missed anything.

'Intelligently' refers to your initial purpose. Reading intelligently will help you distinguish between what you need to know, what you would like to know and what it would be fun to know.

To select what you need to read to fulfil the purpose you set for yourself during your preparation:

▶ *Review the notes you made in Step 1.*
▶ *Add any relevant information you gained as you were reading.*
▶ *Answer the question 'Do I already have what I was looking for?'*
▶ *If you do,* **stop**.
▶ *If you don't, review the key words highlighted during Step 3 – Passive reading, and repeat the question: 'Do I have what I want?'*
▶ *You made notes during Step 4 – Active reading. Review them and again ask whether you have what you want.*
▶ *If you decide that you need more information, go through the book and read the pieces of text you identified as relevant during the first four steps.*
▶ *If you decide you need to read the entire book, you will be able to read it much faster because, having completed the first four steps of the five-step system, you will know what the book contains and what to expect.*

By now you will be familiar with the layout, language and content of the book. You will have spent approximately 40–50 minutes with the book and you will have a good idea of what it contains.

Think carefully again about what exactly you want from the material. The length of time you spend on Step 5 depends on how much you decide you need. Whether you want to read it all or just one paragraph on one page in one chapter, that will be an informed decision and you will not have wasted your time.

## Insight

One of the biggest complaints people make about speed reading books is that they are too big and take too long to read. Use what you learn as you learn it to increase the rate at which you read this book.

## Did you know?

If you know nothing about a subject before you start it is almost impossible to remember what you read. The five-step system helps you build a framework of knowledge, making retention and recall easier.

## Reading for levels of meaning

The purpose of the five-step system is to enable you to gather as much information as possible before you select what you want or have to read. Depending on your material, your reasons and the amount of time you have available, you can use the system in different ways.

The more you understand the **content** of what you are reading, the better your comprehension will be when you read in more depth. The nature of the meaning you gather from applying the five-step system will depend on what you are looking for.

You can get different levels of meaning from a text. Each level requires a different type of reading:

▶ **Literal meaning** – *This is the exact meaning of the text. It mainly consists of facts, figures, dates and names. This information may have to be memorized and it cannot be changed or reinterpreted.*
▶ **Implied meaning** – *This information is not stated directly. It may require analysis. If the author says, 'It was a hot and beautiful day', they imply that the sun was shining for some of that day.*
▶ **Inferred meaning** – *This takes a little more analysis. It requires you to question the author and examine more deeply what they mean.*

> Take this statement: The human mind is like a computer, the trouble is that a computer comes with a manual, our minds don't.

▶ *The **literal meaning** of this sentence is that computers come with manuals.*
▶ *The **implied meaning** is that there is some similarity between the way a computer system works and the way our minds seem to function.*
▶ *The **inferred meaning** is that we know how a computer works because we have a manual as a guide but we will never know how our minds work because we don't have a guide to take us through the intricacies of its functions. If there were a manual we wouldn't have a problem at all.*

Inferred meaning can be as diverse as your imagination. Literal and implied meanings are a little more restricted.

To demonstrate how your reading differs when you look for different levels of meaning, read the following text three times. First, look only for literal meaning; then for implied meaning. Finally read it with your mind wide open, for inferred meaning, giving the text as many different interpretations as you can.

## 'A manager needs to understand that all people are different' by Morris Taylor (printed with the author's permission)

Those who take psychology at degree level will normally study (or at least be in the same room as) what little is known and taught about the topic of Individual Differences – a hopefully self-explanatory term.

They will also explore variations on the theme of classical conditioning (à la Pavlov's Dogs), and they will continue through to – to name a few – behaviourism, social learning, and other important theories about how and why humans behave in particular ways. And perhaps they will learn a little about personality theory and then about how we (mis)behave in groups.

Those who study anthropology – in particular, cultural anthropology – will read about 'Human Universals': those observable (and non-observable) behaviours that can be proven (can we ever?) as occurring in any and every human being or, at the very least, in broad cultural groups.

Could it be that, because of Individual Differences (and, for that matter, cultural differences), there are not as many Human Universals as we might at first think?

Immanuel Kant (who, I hope, will pardon my tongue-in-cheek paraphrasing) said that doing 'good' was only 'good' if it was done for the sake of doing 'good'.

Anton Tolman discussed Haywood: '...true intrinsic motivation is generated by the psychological and internal sensation of dealing with a task "for its own sake ..." '.

John Seddon said '... the big thing that worries me is that when your teacher gives you a gold star, while you might feel good, the other children in the class might feel that they lost out'.

It used to be the case that when psychologists talked about independent variables in their experiments they would discuss among other things 'stimulus materials'. Now we hear more of 'stimulus-in-context'.

Shakespeare said 'Nothing is good or bad except thinking makes it so.'

So could it be that any one out of a set of sticky (?) gold stars on a sheet has little or no meaning except that which we as a group (and thus culturally) choose to import to it? And would that allow me to assert sensibly that the meaning of a gold star has as much to do with cultural influences as it has to do with any other theory of human behaviour? And does whatever meaning we import to a gold star apply universally to everyone who ever gets one even if the contexts are not similar?

Or – as Deming said – is everyone different?

And could 'being different' itself be a behavioural universal?

And that makes me wonder – is there really any difference between a gold star and a red bead ...

I really do wish I knew ... but I don't.

(Source: Morris Taylor (1997),
from discussions on the Deming Electronic Network:
den.list@deming.ces.clemson.edu)

Before you carry on, what was the key idea in the text? Was the author trying to inform, persuade or entertain you? Where was the key sentence? Did the key sentence change depending on what meaning you were looking for?

This exercise emphasizes that you will find what you want to find. It is vital to make sure your purpose is clear.

## Insight

It's human nature to seek out information that supports what we already know and believe. If you really want to challenge your thinking then actively seek out new, interesting and contradictory ideas.

## Reading with a purpose

The more defined your purpose is, the easier your reading will become. Here are a few things to keep in mind as you read that will help you maintain and constantly refine your purpose:

▶ **Application** – *While you read, think of why you are reading the text. When are you going to apply it, what will applying the new information feel like, what will things look like after you have applied it? How much of your own knowledge will be included in what you are learning?*

▶ **Prediction** – *As you read, predict what you think the author is going to say. As a line of argument begins, predict what the outcome might be. You do this naturally when you read a good detective novel. You can do it just as effectively when you read non-fiction. Predict what the author is saying and check your prediction.*

▶ **Interaction** – *Reading is a two-way activity. The author has a message that you could simply accept, but that would not necessarily mean you learned anything new. Interacting with the author is the best way to ensure you learn and are able to apply what you read. Be critical but open-minded about what you read.*

▶ **Solution** – *Many non-fiction books are written as a solution to a problem. This particular book is about speed reading. The problem is 'How can people learn how to read any material they come across easily, quickly and efficiently?' As you read, try to answer the question without waiting for the answer to be revealed to you. Pause for a moment now and ask yourself:*

  ▷ *Based on what I have learnt so far, what can I do now to read faster, more efficiently and more easily that I didn't do beforehand?*

  ▷ *What can I change about the way I think and read that will make reading an enjoyable experience?*

  ▷ *What is good about the way I read now?*

  ▷ *What is ineffective?*

  ▷ *What challenges do I face?*

  ▷ *How can I solve these problems based on what I have learnt so far?*

▶ **Evaluation** – *Take a few moments to stop and summarize what you have learnt from each chapter. As you read the book think how what you learnt in each chapter fits in with the chapter you have just read. The more links you can create between chapters and ideas the better your understanding and recall will be.*

# TEN THINGS TO REMEMBER

1 *Having a clear purpose is the easiest way to cut out the dross and find information you really need.*

2 *Take a minute to prepare your mind and environment before you start to read.*

3 *During the preview stage don't get trapped into reading full paragraphs and sentences all the time.*

4 *Before you start to passive read, make sure your purpose is clear.*

5 *During the active reading stage, avoid getting sucked into reading entire paragraphs and chapters. Set a time of 20 minutes and aim to get through the entire book by only reading the first paragraph of every chapter and the first sentence of every paragraph.*

6 *During the selective reading stage feel free to jump around the book. You don't have to read beginning to end.*

7 *You don't have to finish a book just because you've started it.*

8 *Before you start to read decide how you're going to use the information.*

9 *It's okay to write in books (check that it's yours and that it's not a priceless antique).*

10 *Think for yourself. The author isn't always right.*

# 2

Speed reading

In this chapter you will learn:
- *how to increase your basic reading rate*
- *what a pacer is and how to use it*
- *how to skim and scan*
- *how to get the message*
- *what slows down and speeds up your reading*

Learning to read fast can be challenging. While you learn this improved version of speed reading, a lifetime of habit will constantly interfere with the learning process. You will be developing and securing new habit patterns. Although this will require practice it will be easy and enjoyable because you will see the results immediately.

Speed reading is not just about reading words faster than you did before. It's about being able to read at a speed appropriate for the material you are reading. If you read too slowly your mind will wander, you may become bored and you won't remember anything. If you read too fast you will reduce the chances of remembering what you want to remember, you will become frustrated and stressed and thus even less likely to remember.

The more flexible you are with your reading, the faster you will be able to read and the more information you will retain.

If you want to increase your reading rate and increase your comprehension, then it is important to read often. The more you read, the better you will become at recognizing when you can read fast and when to slow down.

## Factors contributing to speed

▶ **Clarity of purpose** – *Step 1 of the five-step system is preparation. Always know why you are reading something. The clearer your purpose, the faster you will be able to read.*

▶ **Mood** – *If you are feeling tired, restless, impatient or irritable you are unlikely to be able to read as quickly as when you are alert, fresh, happy and relaxed. However, you may not always be alert, fresh, happy and relaxed when you have to read. Learning how to recognize and manage your feelings so that you can concentrate regardless of how you might be feeling at the time is not always easy. There are some guidelines in Chapter 4 that may help.*

▶ **Familiarity with the subject-related terminology** – *If you are already familiar with the subject you will have a framework on which to build. You will not have to stop to think about what the words might mean and you are more likely to be able to read quite quickly.*

▶ **Difficulty of the text** – *Some books are difficult to read even if you are familiar with the terminology and content.*

▶ **Urgency and stress levels** – *Do you notice that when you absolutely have to read something immediately, you can't read quickly? Stress will slow you down. The chapters on concentration and memory (Chapters 4 and 5) will look at stress more closely and offer ways for you to reduce your stress levels.*

### Insight

If you're in a bad mood don't try to read anything even remotely important, technical or that you'll have to voice an opinion on. Your mood will taint that opinion and you might well say something you'll regret.

Factors affecting learning to read quickly:

▶ *A good attitude towards reading. A desire to learn how you can improve your reading and consider what it is that you will get from speed reading.*

▶ *Familiarity with the language related to the subject and a good vocabulary.*

▶ *Good background knowledge of the subject or, if you do not have that yet, a strategy for building the background knowledge quickly.*

▶ *Don't bother setting time aside each day to 'practise' speed reading. Just use these techniques on everything you read, all the time.*

## Real people

In the middle of an exercise during a speed reading class one of the students suddenly put down his book, sat back and folded his arms, annoyed. I asked him what was wrong. He shrugged, looked at the individual next to him and said, 'He's reading faster than I am.' For the rest of the session he sat at the back of the room and read a newspaper.

Speed reading is a very personal practice. Everyone reads with different levels of knowledge and experience. Even if you are learning with someone else you will probably learn at different rates. Avoid comparing your skill with anyone else's.

There are many ways to pick out information at varying speeds. Reading every word in a book or article is only necessary if you have a specific reason for doing so. Before you decide whether you need to do this, you need to know what information the reading material contains. After you have gone through Steps 1 to 4 of Chapter 1 (preparation, preview, passive reading and active reading), you will be ready to select what you want to read in more depth. Now is the time to speed read.

---

## Where are you now?

Before you can improve something you need to know your starting point. That will help you to establish what will be required to take you where you want to go. One way to do this is to ask yourself these three questions:

▶ *Where am I now?*
▶ *Where do I want to get to?*
▶ *How will I know when I have got there?*

To put these questions another way:

▶ *How fast do you currently read?*
▶ *How fast do you want to read?*
▶ *How will you know when you have reached your goal?*

It is not easy to determine accurately how fast you read; everything you read is different. Each piece of material is written with varying levels of complexity and you will be reading each one with a different purpose. To determine an average reading rate, you need to read more than one type of text.

For the purpose of this exercise, gather together six different types of material you might read. The examples should vary in complexity but you should be familiar with the subjects of each. If you do not have appropriate material to hand and you would still like an estimate of your reading speed, note that a piece of suitable text has been included in Chapter 11 as a speed practice test. The extract is from *The Energy Advantage* by Dr Chris Fenn (see pp. 169–176).

## MEASURING YOUR READING RATE

Read through this procedure before starting to measure your own rate:

1  *Gather all your reading materials or go to Chapter 11.*
2  *Set a timer for* **2 minutes** *(although you are working out your reading rate in terms of words per minute, you will need time to warm up; 1 minute does not give you the time but 2 minutes will).*
3  *Then, reading as you normally read, without doing anything differently at all, read for* **good comprehension** *for 2 minutes.*
4  *When the timer stops you:*
   ▷  *count the number of words on three full lines of text;*
   ▷  *divide the total number by 3;*
   ▷  *count the number of lines you read;*
   ▷  *multiply the number of lines by the average number of words per line.*
   *Example: Number of words on 3 full lines = 30*
   *Divided by 3 for average words/line = 10*
   *If you read 50 lines (50 × 10) = 500*
5  *Divide that figure by 2 (remember you are looking for your words per minute reading rate; you read for 2 minutes so you need to divide the number you calculated above by 2).*
   *Example: Divide final figure by 2 (500 ÷ 2) = 250*
6  *That figure is your average reading rate for the text you read.*
7  *If you have chosen your own material, do the same with all six texts you gathered so that you have a words per minute (WPM) rate for all six texts.*
8  *Then add all the final WPMs together and divide the result by 6. This will give you a reflection of your current reading rate across a number of different texts.*
9  *Plot your reading rate on the graph at the end of this chapter.*
10 *Finally, check your comprehension. If you read the extract from* The Energy Advantage *answer the questions provided. If you used your own texts, take a few minutes to recall what you can from each text. Check your information against the sections you read.*

Remember to fill in the date and, more important, the time of day you read. At certain times of day you read better than at other times. When you have charted your speed reading progress for a week you might begin to notice a pattern. If possible, read material that requires maximum concentration at one of the times you identify as being most productive.

Plotting your reading rate will give you an indication of your speed reading progress. If your reading rate begins to drop at any point, your progress graph will tell you at what times of the day you are reading most effectively.

Stop reading this book now and determine your current reading rate, using either the six texts of your choice or the text in Chapter 11.

## Comparison exercise

If you read the extract from *The Energy Advantage* you can do a comparison exercise. When you have finished reading and have answered as many questions as you can, read the questions you didn't or couldn't answer, then go through the text again. This time the purpose of reading is to find the answers to the questions. Remember to time yourself.

After you have done that, consider the following questions:

▶ *What strategy did you use?*
▶ *Were you looking for key words?*
▶ *Did you read more than was required for each answer?*
▶ *Were you satisfied that you found the full answer before moving on?*
▶ *How much faster did you move through the text the second time compared to the first time you read it?*
▶ *Was the reading easier when you had a clearly defined purpose or did you find you were still tempted to read more than was required?*

## Increasing your basic reading rate

Two of the main reasons we tend to read slowly are that:

▶ *We read with our ears instead of with our eyes (more on this in Chapter 7).*
▶ *We are easily distracted by what is on the page and by what is going on around us.*

### THE PACER

A simple tool that will help you eliminate many of your speed reading problems is a pacer. A pacer can be your finger, a chopstick, a pencil or pen – anything you can use to help you focus your attention on the words on the page by moving it as you read.

A pacer helps to eliminate most distractions, and it involves an extra sense in the reading process. Using a pacer adds a kinaesthetic, physical dimension to your reading. You are actually doing something as well as simply reading. You are involving your hands as well.

Using a pacer helps your reading in several ways:

▶ *It encourages your eyes to focus on more than one word at a time – this immediately increases your reading rate.*
▶ *The pacer focuses you on what you are reading instead of allowing your eyes to jump around the page at anything that attracts your attention.*

## An experiment

Here is an experiment for you to try. Find someone willing to take part. Ask that person to draw a circle in the air using their eyes. Notice the eye movements. Are they smooth or jerky? Do they create a full circle or does it look like they

*(Contd)*

are cutting curves? Next, ask them to draw a circle in the air with their own finger and this time to follow their finger with their own eyes. Watch their eyes. This time, do you notice that their eyes are moving smoothly, quickly and deliberately?

A pacer will also help you:

▶ *Move to new lines smoothly and easily.*
▶ *Prevent you losing your place.*
▶ *Prevent excessive sub-vocalization (the voice inside your head caused by reading with your ears) by speeding up the pace at which you read and allowing you to see more than one word at a time.*

## How to use a pacer

Place your pacer on the first word on the line and move it smoothly across the page to the end of the line, then return it to the next line.

Use your pacer to read the boxed paragraph. Place the pacer on the dotted line and move it smoothly along the line across the page. Re-read this paragraph several times until you feel that you have the rhythm smooth and fast – also, move the pacer just a little bit quicker than you **think** you can read.

What was different about reading with a pacer? How did you feel? How much faster did you feel you read? How do you feel about comprehension?

It is important that the pacer moves smoothly and steadily across the page.

_____

If the movement is hesitant your eyes are dictating the pace at which you

_____

read and your reading rate will not increase. If the pacer moves smoothly,

_____

your eyes, with practice, will learn to keep up and your brain will learn to

_____

absorb the meaning of groups of words in a new way.

_____

Practise the above **at least** ten times to get used to the rhythm.

## Insight

Are you reading with a pacer? If not, start now. Use a pacer to read the remainder of this book. By the time you have finished the book, using the pacer will have become a habit and you will be well on the way to becoming an expert speed reader.

### DIFFERENT TYPES OF PACING

The pacing you are using now is one basic method for guiding your eye across the page. There are different methods of pacing for different types of material and reader needs.

### Technical material with which you are unfamiliar

Place the pacer under every line and move it steadily across the page from the beginning to the end of each line. This method ensures that you miss nothing.

### Technical material that you are familiar with

Place your pacer under every second line. This method encourages you to read more than one line at a time.

Look at the space in front of you. Notice that your view is quite wide. When you learned how to read you were taught to focus on only one thing at a time instead of being encouraged to see what you are capable of seeing in a single glance. Reading more than one line at a time comes with practice. In Chapter 7 we explore the eyes and how they work. You will find an exercise in that chapter (pp. 120–121) that will help you read more than one line at a time.

### Very familiar material

If you are very familiar with the reading material, and if you only need to have a general idea about what you are reading, you can run the pacer down either the side or the middle of the page.

Ultimately, the more you experiment, the more flexible your reading will become and you will develop the ability to change from one technique to another as you read.

Hints to increase your speed:

▶ **Push yourself** – *It is easy to stay in a comfort zone of reading slowly. Once you break through the barrier of believing that you can only remember what you read when you hear every word, your enjoyment of reading and your pace will increase.*

▶ **Practise often** – *Use everything you read as a practice medium. Speed read the information on bottle labels or the blurb on the back of a cereal packet. Instead of just reading as you have previously, read with the purpose of practising reading as fast as you can for good comprehension. Use a pacer.*

▶ **Build the context first** – *The first four steps of the five-step system (see Chapter 1) will make it easier to speed read anything you read, and to do that several times faster than if you were reading it for the first time.*

- **The faster you go the less you will vocalize** – *In the next section, on skimming and scanning, we shall discuss building speed and maintaining it. Play with these exercises daily until you feel that they are a natural part of your reading strategy.*
- **Eliminate or decrease distractions** – *In Chapter 8 we shall discuss distractions and suggest some solutions to them that will allow you to concentrate more easily. The more you are able to concentrate, the faster you will be able to read.*
- **Read actively** – *The techniques you use during Step 4 (active reading) should be used while you speed read in Step 5 (selective reading). Take notes, mark and highlight relevant sections, make comments as you read, build mind-maps (explained on pp. 80–81) and think about the arguments as you read. If you must do any talking inside your head while you read, choose to make it a debate or dialogue on aspects of the topic with the author. The more actively you read, the better your understanding and long-term comprehension will be.*

## Important things to remember about speed reading

Speed reading is not just reading fast all the time. The technical content of the material, the print size, your familiarity with the subject and, particularly, your **purpose** in reading can affect the speed at which you read. The key to speed reading is having the choice to read as fast or as slow as you wish.

Now re-read the instructions for measuring your reading rate (p. 25) and follow them to take another speed reading measurement. Use the pacing technique.

## Skimming and scanning

In this section we consider skimming and scanning:

▶ *What are they and what is the difference between them?*
▶ *When should we use them?*

The difference between skimming and scanning is that when you **scan** for information you are looking for something very specific, for example a telephone number or an answer to a particular question. You generally stop once you have it. **Skimming** is used when you are seeking more of a general impression of what the text is about. You could skim a whole text if you wanted to, but you would probably not skim a whole telephone directory to find your number.

## Try this experiment

In the following piece of text there are six Japanese words – you have 45 seconds to find them:

The history of speed reading dates back to the beginning of the century when the volume of printed material exploded. This resulted aiki in the abandonment of the notion of idle reading. More information engulfed readers of the time far faster than they could read it.

The first development in speed reading came from the Royal Air Force, believe it or not! Pilots needed to be trained to spot enemy planes before they went into battle, training took place on a barcos device called a tachistoscope. The machine flashed bugei an image of the plane at the pilot for a fraction of a second and the time allowed became smaller and smaller; they found that after a while the pilots were able to recognize enemy planes from far greater distances at far greater speeds than they did before. The technology was transferred to the study of reading. First a single word was flashed on the tachistoscope, then two then three and four remar words were flashed at a time. Reading rates increased to about 400 words a minute with the aid of the machine. The great drawback of the tachistoscope was hyung that it was not portable. Once people stopped practising dasu on it their reading rates dropped rapidly.

It was believed for a long alquiler time since those first experiments that 400 w.p.m. was the fastest nekuru possible reading speed. But we have come to realize that we are capable of far more than we ever thought possible – in fact we have no idea what the fastest possible reading rate is because we still don't understand the zuki infinite capacity of our minds.

▸ *Did you find the six Japanese words in 45 seconds?*
▸ *Did you find any Spanish words as well? (There are three in the passage.)*
▸ *Did you find a word and realize it wasn't English but it wasn't Japanese either and move on without counting it, or did you just look for six foreign words?*
▸ *Did you pick up any meaning from the text?*
▸ *Did 'tachistoscope' get your attention?*
▸ *Did you notice the factual error in the first paragraph?*

## For your information

Japanese words in the text: *aiki, bugei, hyung, dasu, nekuru, zuki*

Spanish words in the text: *barcos, remar, alquiler*

What you have just done is **scanning**. As already explained, this technique is used when you are looking for specific information such as an answer to a particular question or a telephone number in a directory. You have to know exactly what you are looking for. If you don't know Japanese or Spanish it would have been very difficult for you to determine which language the foreign words belong to. You also probably didn't spot the factual error in the first paragraph because you weren't looking for it.

**Skimming**, however, is reading with a different purpose. This time, spend 45 seconds on the text to find out what it is generally about. Don't read it word for word, just 'skim' over the text, reading enough to *get the message*.

How did you do?

- *Did you notice all nine foreign words? You probably glanced at them and then moved on.*
- *How much of the text did you read and how much did you drift over?*
- *Are you satisfied that you have a general idea of what the text is about?*
- *What else did you pick up? This time, did you notice the factual error in the first paragraph?*
- *Did 'tachistoscope' get your attention?*

Skimming is used during Step 3 of the five-step system (passive reading). You use skimming when you know what you are looking for and want a general impression of what the text contains.

There are different types of skimming to use depending on what your purpose is:

- *Skimming to overview – The purpose of this method is to get an outline of what the material is about. You will be looking more at structure than content. This method is used mostly in Step 2 (preview) of the five-step system.*
- *Skimming to preview – This is used when you know you are going to re-read the material. Your purpose is to gather*

*as much background information as you can on the subject without spending too much time on it.*

▶ *Skimming to review – You would use this method when you have already read the material and your purpose is to re-familiarize yourself with the content.*

### SUCCESSFUL SKIMMING

Skimming for information is easier when you know where the information is likely to be within the overall scheme of the piece you are reading. While you are speed reading look for the core information. Once you have clarified your purpose for skimming and you know what you are looking for, you will be able to identify trigger words that hold the relevant information, such as the following:

▶ *who*
▶ *what*
▶ *where*
▶ *why*
▶ *when*
▶ *how.*

The following words pre-empt a contradiction or argument against the case:

▶ *but*
▶ *none the less*
▶ *however*
▶ *yet*
▶ *on the other hand.*

## Practice box

Practise using these words by going through newspaper or magazine articles with the purpose of identifying the 5Ws and how, and any contradictions, as quickly as you can.

## Speed reading and getting the message

When you read you convert the information embedded in groups of words into ideas, images, thoughts, feelings and actions. One purpose of reading is to get the message from the words. This does not necessarily mean you have to read all the words. When you speed read – especially when you start to read more than one line at a time – you may initially become confused because the words are presented to you in order different from that intended. When you read with your eyes you will find that this does not present a problem because your brain works out what the sentence means, regardless of what order the words are in.

Your brain is always trying to make sense of information it receives. When the information you are reading is not complete your brain will naturally fill in the blanks and organize the information so that you can make sense of it. First, read the following sentences **out loud** and work out what they mean:

▶ *We'll twenty minutes in be there.*
▶ *Let's dinner for tonight go out.*
▶ *Reading visual activity done slowly is only the.*

Now look at the next batch of sentences and get the meaning from them as quickly as you can by looking at the whole sentence and identifying the key words:

▶ *Speed reading have if you a purpose is easy.*
▶ *Have yet holiday you been on this year?*
▶ *The improve is to best way to practise.*

Which was quicker, reading with your ears or reading with your eyes?

You don't have to have the words in the right order to get the message.

### *MAKING SURE YOU GET THE RIGHT MESSAGE*

What if you speed read a text using all the skimming and scanning methods you know and get the message, only to find that you have missed out one crucial word that changes the entire meaning of the passage?

> In the following sentence:
>
> An effective speed reader never reads without something to write with, always reads with a purpose and never reads every word.
>
> If you miss out the word 'never', you get:
>
> An effective speed reader reads without something to write with, always reads with a purpose and reads every word.

The sentence makes sense but the message is contrary to that intended. Practice, a clear purpose and using the five-step system will help you understand the meaning.

---

## Bilingual speed readers

One challenge for bilingual readers is wanting to develop speed reading skills in their new language before they are totally fluent. Also the reading they might be required to do may be fairly complex.

I have had foreign students in my classes who could speak their second language fluently but had become highly frustrated with themselves because they were unable to read their second language as fast as their first language. Speaking a second language is different from reading. You can choose the words you use when you speak, but not the words you read in a new passage.

Speed reading a second language is full of challenges. The first is vocabulary. Another aspect of reading a second language that will slow you down is translating into your first language as you go. As long as you do this you will not be able to reach high speeds.

There are a few things you can do to begin increasing your reading rate for a foreign language:

▶ *Learn the roots, suffixes and prefixes of the new language.*
▶ *Practise speed reading techniques on very simple books.*
  ▷ *Select a few children's books and speed read them using tools and techniques you are presently developing.*
  ▷ *Avoid moving to another level until you are comfortable with the speed at which you are reading and sure that you understand what you are reading without having to translate it into your first language. When you can do that you are ready to move on to more complex material.*
▶ *For practice, use the five-step system with every book, even novels. This will give you an overall picture of what you are reading and will make comprehension much easier.*
▶ *Read as many novels as you can. The story will often distract you from the complexity of the language.*
▶ *Set out with the intent of enjoying the learning process. Frustration causes stress and slows you down.*

## Exercises to increase your speed reading rate and flexibility

For all the following exercises, use books you are looking forward to reading. Even if the books are on subjects you are unfamiliar with, make sure you are interested in those subjects.

When you are comfortable with the different exercises, begin using material that you enjoy reading less. This may include some material you have to read for work or study that you are not particularly interested in. While practising on such material make sure that you set very firm time limits. If you don't you will become bored and want to move on to something else.

Treat these exercises as games and challenges. Don't do them for any more than 10 minutes at a time unless you really want to.

### WARM-UP STRETCHING

This is a short five-minute warm-up exercise:

▶ *Read for good comprehension for* **one minute.**
▶ *Put a mark at the point you reached.*
▶ *Add half a page to what you have already read and mark that point.*
▶ *Now go back to the beginning and read (for good comprehension) to the second mark in* **one minute.**
▶ **Make sure you make your mark.**
▶ *Once you are comfortable reaching the second mark add another half page and read from the beginning to the third mark in* **one minute.**
▶ *Add another half page. Read to the fourth mark in* **one minute.**
▶ *Add another half page. Read to the fifth mark in* **one minute.**

▶ *If at this point you find that you are not 'reading', keep in mind that that is the point of this exercise. Make sure that you see every word just sufficiently to recognize that it is an English word. This exercise will help you get used to seeing/ recognizing more than one word at a time.*

## STRETCHING SPEED AND COMPREHENSION

This quick exercise will help improve your memory and increase your speed:

1 *Using a pacer, read one page as fast as you can.*
2 *Stop and write down everything you remember from what you just read.*
3 *Read five pages like this every day, gradually increasing the number of pages you read before you stop to recall what you read.*
4 *Start with a subject familiar to you, then – as you notice that your ability, confidence and comfort are improving – take on more challenging material.*

The next stage is as follows:

5 *Read for one minute and count how many lines you have read.*
6 *Continue reading for another minute, reading* **two lines more** *than you did the first time.*
7 *In the next minute read four lines more than you did in the first minute, then six, then eight, then ten.*
8 *Always read for* **good comprehension and recall.** *As soon as you think you don't understand or remember the text, consolidate at that level until you are comfortable, then speed up gradually.*

Reading quickly requires concentration. If you don't understand or remember what you read you may find your concentration drifting because you are becoming disappointed and perhaps bored.

As your concentration improves, stretch yourself by extending the 1-minute trip to 2 minutes, then to 4, and 6, and 8 ... and so on.

## FINDING KEY SENTENCES

This technique is good for the parts of the text that you are already fairly familiar with when you just want to be sure you have missed nothing out:

▶ Read the **first** sentence of the paragraph.
▶ Skim the rest of the paragraph for key words and if necessary read the **last** sentence of the paragraph.

## INCREASING SPEED FLEXIBILITY

To improve your flexibility:

▶ Select a text on a subject familiar to you.
▶ Start reading slowly at first, almost word for word.
▶ As you finish the first paragraph, speed up your reading rate until you are reading as fast as you can for good comprehension.
▶ Once you think you are beginning to read faster than you can comprehend, slow down a bit.
▶ Then begin to practise flexible reading. To do this, read the first sentence of the paragraph relatively slowly and speed up as you go through the paragraph, only slowing down when you come to sections you are not familiar with.
▶ When you have read a book on a familiar subject for a while, change to a book on an unfamiliar subject and start again.
▶ Compare the two experiences. What did you notice? Did you find that reading the familiar book was much easier than reading the unfamiliar book? Did the speed at which you read the unfamiliar book increase as you began to notice what was easier or more challenging to read?

## Practice box – novel exercise

Novels are a good source of practice to develop flexibility in pacing. At the start of the novel you might find that you pace under every line; as you get familiar with the plot you might pace under every two lines. When the story really gets going and you are looking for the exciting bits in between the description you might find that you run the pacer down the middle of the page until you come to the sections of the book that really carry the story. Your enjoyment of the book is not lessened in any way at all; in fact you may find that you actually finish more novels than you used to.

### METRONOME PACING

You can buy a small electronic metronome (ideally one with a 'tick' that is not too loud) at any music store quite cheaply – it will be a good investment.

Do this exercise for 2 minutes, then relax for 5 minutes:

1 *Set the metronome at its slowest speed and read one line per 'tick'.*
2 *Every page or half page increase the pace of the metronome by one tick, or more if you are comfortable about it.*
3 *Then relax.*
4 *Repeat this until you reach the fastest speed on the metronome.*

The metronome will reach a speed at which you will not be able to read every word. This exercise 'pushes' your eye and brain to see and absorb more than one word at a time, and gradually stretches your ability.

If you drive on a motorway at 70 miles per hour and as you approach a town you suddenly have to reduce your speed to 30 m.p.h., you might think you are travelling at 30 until the police stop you and inform you that you were travelling at 40 or 50 – much faster than you thought. The similarity between driving and speed reading doesn't stop there. When travelling at 70 m.p.h. you have to concentrate and don't have time to look at the scenery. When speed reading you are reading so fast that your mind doesn't want to wander as much as it can at '30 m.p.h.'.

## Insight

This is a great exercise but it might get into your head! You'll read a novel and the tick will appear. A newspaper… a tick. The metronome will loom large in your imagination, so increase the pace of your imaginary ticker and use it to increase your reading rate accordingly.

## Speed reading graph

| Reading speed | | | | | | | | | | | | | | | | | | | | | |
|---|---|---|---|---|---|---|---|---|---|---|---|---|---|---|---|---|---|---|---|---|---|
| | | | | | | | | | | | | | | | | | | | | | |
| | | | | | | | | | | | | | | | | | | | | | |
| | | | | | | | | | | | | | | | | | | | | | |
| | | | | | | | | | | | | | | | | | | | | | |
| 1101–1200 | | | | | | | | | | | | | | | | | | | | | |
| 1001–1100 | | | | | | | | | | | | | | | | | | | | | |
| 901–1000 | | | | | | | | | | | | | | | | | | | | | |
| 801–900 | | | | | | | | | | | | | | | | | | | | | |
| 701–800 | | | | | | | | | | | | | | | | | | | | | |
| 601–700 | | | | | | | | | | | | | | | | | | | | | |
| 501–600 | | | | | | | | | | | | | | | | | | | | | |
| 401–500 | | | | | | | | | | | | | | | | | | | | | |
| 351–400 | | | | | | | | | | | | | | | | | | | | | |
| 301–350 | | | | | | | | | | | | | | | | | | | | | |
| 251–300 | | | | | | | | | | | | | | | | | | | | | |
| 201–250 | | | | | | | | | | | | | | | | | | | | | |
| 150–200 | | | | | | | | | | | | | | | | | | | | | |
| Date/time → | | | | | | | | | | | | | | | | | | | | | |

As well as providing you with information on your speed reading progress, the speed reading graph will help you to remain motivated. Put as much information into it as you need. Measure your reading rate for the duration of your 21-day programme (see Chapter 12, What next?, pp. 178–185).

▶ *In the bottom row enter the date and time when measuring your reading.*

▶ *Each time you measure how many words per minute you are reading place a mark in the appropriate box. Add any thoughts or ideas about your progress in a notebook specifically kept for your reading development.*

▶ *When your reading rate surpasses 1200, write your own numbers in the blank spaces above 1101–1200 to record it.*

▶ *Take speed reading measurements at different times of the day and under different conditions (these include mood, time pressure and so on).*

# TEN THINGS TO REMEMBER

1 *Speed reading takes practice. Getting it right comes from a combination of knowing your purpose, how you're going to use information and having faith that you'll spot what you need.*

2 *The speed at which you can read is determined by factors including clarity of purpose, your mood, familiarity with jargon, deadlines, your environment and how bright the sun is shining outside.*

3 *Everyone reads at different speeds. Don't compare your progress to anyone else.*

4 *Use a pacer as you read. It keeps your attention on the page and your eyes moving.*

5 *For as long as you insist on reading word for word you will only ever be able to read as fast as you can speak.*

6 *Speed reading is really only glorified skimming.*

7 *Knowing your purpose will make sure you find what you need.*

8 *Eliminate as many distractions as you can.*

9 *Speed reading non-fiction will not ruin your love of fiction.*

10 *Speed reading is more about getting what the author is saying than remembering exactly what he or she has written word for word.*

# 3

It's all in the words – developing your vocabulary

In this chapter you will learn:
- **the different types of vocabulary**
- **how to increase your vocabulary**
- **how words are made up**
- **how to deal with specialized vocabulary**

## Why increasing your vocabulary speeds up your reading

The bigger your vocabulary, the faster you will be able to read. Unfamiliar words will slow you down because you'll naturally start asking yourself questions like, 'What does it mean?', 'Does it change the context?', 'Is it important to my understanding of the text?'. Although these questions might fly through your mind, by the time you've answered them you would almost certainly have forgotten what you've read. As a result, the real time waster will be going back to the beginning of the text to remind yourself of what you read.

You have three different levels of vocabulary knowledge available to you; your spoken vocabulary (generally the most limited of the three), your written vocabulary and your recognized vocabulary (the largest of the three). Most people use between 2,000 and 12,000 words in speech. Written vocabulary is bigger than spoken vocabulary because you have more time to think about what you want to say and can go over what you have written and edit your text until you are happy with it. Most people use between 2,000 and 25,000 different words in their lifetime for writing. By far the largest set of vocabulary you have at your disposal is your recognized vocabulary. This is the words you recognize within a context but do not ordinarily use. Words you recognize are sometimes difficult to define clearly. You have a sense that you know what the word means in the context that you read or heard it, but cannot define it clearly.

Your recognized vocabulary is also known as 'passive' vocabulary – you know the words but don't use them. Written and spoken vocabulary is your 'active' vocabulary.

The aim of this chapter is to help you convert your passive vocabulary into active vocabulary, not to learn the most obscure words in the language so that you baffle or bore your friends and ever-decreasing audience of listeners. Instead, learn your chosen language so you can express your ideas and understand others clearly and precisely.

## How to increase your vocabulary

There are several ways to increase your vocabulary. You should approach them gradually rather than deciding that you want to learn 1,000 new words in one day and locking yourself in a room until you have. Unless you happen to learn best that way (and have the time and genuine inclination to do it) there are other, more useful strategies.

A better way of extending your vocabulary may be to break the exercise up into 30-minute chunks. Picking five words a day from the dictionary might not work for everyone. The following are a few different ways of increasing your vocabulary. Your choice will be determined by how you like to gather information:

> ▶ *If you like reading a lot (and you have the time), then read books with complicated language. Use a dictionary as you*

go but before you look an unfamiliar word up try to figure out what it means yourself. This way you will learn the language as you go. Make a note of the new words you learn as you do this.

▶ If reading is not your favourite activity but communicating and speaking to people is, then aim to meet people who you know have a good vocabulary and talk to them. You can pick up a lot in conversation. If you hear a word you do not understand but don't want to ask the person who says it what it means, then make a mental note to look it up later. It is worth remembering that many people use a word because they know it fits the context but do not really know what the word means. If you hear a particularly obscure word think twice about asking for a definition; the speaker might feel awkward if they are not entirely sure about its meaning.

▶ A third way of increasing your vocabulary is to use new language. Pick a word a day and use it whenever it is appropriate. Try not to make it obvious that you are trying out a new word by using it in every sentence unless you are in an environment where you can relax and play with language.

▶ A good way to increase your active awareness of language is to carry a vocabulary notebook with you. Whenever you hear or read a word that you do not understand or that is unfamiliar, write down the word, your understanding of it and the context you heard or read it in. Then, when you have the chance, look the word up to check whether your guess was accurate. This is an especially good exercise for turning passive vocabulary into active vocabulary; it encourages you to think about the definition of a word you think you know the meaning of.

▶ Relax while you learn. If you get a word wrong, don't worry about it. The more you practise, read and use new language in conversation, the better your vocabulary will become.

▶ Use your imagination while you learn new language. Imagine yourself using a new word and think about the response you *might expect if you used it inappropriately. Imagine what the word might mean, basing that on your knowledge of other words. Imagine what the word would mean if you could give it any definition you like. Take time to play with language.*

## The source of it all – roots, suffixes and prefixes

One of the easiest ways of learning more language and of becoming able to recognize new words and work out their meaning is by learning how words are made up.

### Did you know?

A quarter of the words in the English language come directly from other languages. This accounts for the diverse spelling of many words we use. However, much of the English language originates in Latin or Greek. The roots, suffixes and prefixes that form the basis of our language are almost all Latin and Greek. How much easier it is to learn a new word if you know the roots of the word. Here is a fact you might not be aware of: 22 roots and 13 prefixes are found in 100,000 words in an unabridged dictionary. That means that if you know 22 roots and 13 prefixes you may be able to work out the meaning of 100,000 words.

In Chapter 11 there is a table of roots, suffixes and prefixes (pp. 164–167). Carry the prefixes/suffixes and roots table around with you for a few weeks . Instead of looking up an unfamiliar word in the dictionary, try to use your knowledge of prefixes, suffixes and roots to work out the meaning of the word.

> During Step 3 (passive reading) and Step 4 (active reading) of
> the five-step system look for unfamiliar words as part of the
> skimming exercise, then look them up before you begin Step 5
> (selective reading).

## Specialized vocabulary

Developing an understanding of specialized vocabulary needs to be
dealt with in a way different from normal vocabulary. Generally,
words you do not understand in the text make sense within the
context of the sentence. Usually you can read on without knowing
exactly what a word means; you will still understand what the
sentence or paragraph means. Not understanding specialized
language can make it impossible to understand any of the text,
especially if the entire piece revolves around that one word.

The more familiar you are with the specialized text, the faster
you will be able to read. Becoming familiar with the text might
take some time depending on the level of knowledge you already
have. If you follow a few simple steps, the learning process can
become much easier.

▶ *During Step 3 (passive reading),* **highlight** *all the words you do
  not understand especially if they look as if they may be part of
  a specialist vocabulary.*
▶ *If you are allowed, copy the* **glossary** *from the book (if there
  is one). If there isn't, use a good* **specialist dictionary** *(most
  subjects have one – if not a hard copy, then on the Internet). If
  the dictionary belongs to you, you could highlight each word
  you had difficulty with. Alternatively, when working from
  a dictionary you could write the word in a separate book or
  place markers on the pages so that you can go back and find
  the definition quickly again.*
▶ *Once you are familiar with the vocabulary, take a bit of time
  to* **think** *how each word fits in with any ideas you have on the*

subject. Think about how else you could use the vocabulary. Consider how the word is made up. Does the root, suffix or prefix give you an idea of what the meaning could be? In what other context might you come across the word?

▶ If you have the time, look up the specialist vocabulary in an **ordinary dictionary**. You may be surprised by differences in meaning and interpretation from those in the specialist dictionary. Do this especially if you do not understand the definition in the specialist dictionary. Very often, a level of knowledge is assumed in the specialist dictionary and definitions may not be complete. An ordinary dictionary assumes a bare knowledge of the subject, so if the word is in one, the definition may be more helpful. **Encyclopaedic dictionaries** are good because they very often have pictures next to the definition. You can explore and have fun with these.

▶ Can you find a **picture** that illustrates the word? If so, remembering the definition will be easier.

▶ The more you read on the subject, the more familiar you will become with the language of the subject.

## If that doesn't work ...

... and if you still have problems with specialist language, attend as many talks and lectures on the subject as you can. Speak to experts on the subject and, instead of asking them only what a word means (you will more than likely get a dictionary definition), ask them how the word fits into the subject as a whole.

# TEN THINGS TO REMEMBER

1 *Have a dictionary close by because few things slow you down more than stumbling over words you don't understand.*

2 *The bigger your vocabulary the more comfortable you will feel about reading fast.*

3 *The best way to increase your vocabulary is to not let a single word that you don't understand go by without investigation (in reading, and in conversation).*

4 *If someone uses technical or specialized terminology, ask them what they mean.*

5 *In a work environment, especially if you're new to a company, always ask the meaning of jargon and acronyms. Keep a note of them to hand.*

6 *Build subject specific personal dictionaries related to your field of interest and work.*

7 *Learn a new language. It will help you examine the structure of your own language and there are few joys greater than being able to travel unfettered by linguistic ignorance.*

8 *Use new words you pick up.*

9 *Learn the structure of words. It will help you work out what they mean.*

10 *To get a good grasp of specialized language immerse yourself in the subject on all levels: books, Internet, lectures, conversations.*

# 4

## Concentration

In this chapter you will learn:
* *the importance of concentration*
* *the different types of concentration*
* *tips for improving your concentration*
* *exercises to increase concentration*

### The importance of concentration

### Insight

Our determination to know everything opens us to massive quantities of information, most of which we don't need and is probably untrue, exaggerated or unsubstantiated. The more you *choose* the information presented to you, the easier it will be to sift through the nonsense and concentrate on what's relevant.

The first rule of acquiring knowledge: Pay attention.

Without concentration there is no memory. Some ideas on how to concentrate and avoid the distractions that break up your concentration will be presented in Chapter 8, Distractions and solutions.

Concentration does not come easily to many, for two reasons:

1 *We can be very easily distracted.*
2 *There can be much to distract us.*

Improving concentration isn't easy. We certainly do not always have either the time or desire to meditate and practise absolute concentration for several hours each day. Fortunately, there are other ways to achieve better concentration skills.

### FOCUSED ATTENTION

Attention has certain definite properties:

- *It is **dynamic**. Try focusing on one thing only and notice how long it is before your mind wanders. The aim of meditation is to enable you to focus on one element of something without losing attention. People train and practise for years to achieve this.*
- *Attention is **undivided**. If you tried to listen to more than one conversation at a time or to read a book and drive a car simultaneously you would find that fairly challenging.*
- *Attention follows **interest**. Boredom will extinguish attention in a moment. Always keep in mind 'What is in it for me?'*
- *Attention is maintained by a series of **discoveries**. Be aware of what is new about what you are learning. How often do you get that 'Aha!' feeling?*

Sometimes we have to force ourselves to pay attention. This can be unpleasant and ineffective since attention lasts for only a few seconds in those circumstances and has to be constantly reinforced.

There are several kinds of attention:

- **Voluntary attention** – *This is what you display when you are totally absorbed by what you are doing and distracted by nothing. When you voluntarily pay attention to something you do so naturally. You don't have to force yourself to concentrate; you find yourself absorbed in the task.*
- **Autopilot** – *This occurs when you find yourself at your destination but do not know how you got there. It also happens when you reach the end of a book and realize you*

*have not remembered anything although you know you read every word.*

▶ **Dispersed attention** – *Unfortunately most of us suffer from this more than we would like. Having too many things going on simultaneously causes dispersed attention, as does a lack of interest. When this happens you feel as though you cannot concentrate at all, everything attracts your attention and you can't focus on anything for longer than a few moments.*

The aim is to be able to control voluntary attention so that even in situations where you would normally find it difficult to concentrate you are able to focus your attention willingly and fully.

### DIVIDED ATTENTION – WHEN IT WORKS AND WHEN IT DOESN'T

Attention is a linear activity. If you are already carrying out a task using one sense or if you are doing something that requires a high level of attention, you will be able to do only one thing at a time. For instance, if you are driving in dangerous conditions you will notice that your attention to driving is total. If the radio is on, you will probably not hear it. If, on the other hand, the road is clear and the conditions are good, you may be able to drive, listen to the radio and have a conversation at the same time. The moment a dog runs into the road your attention will shift entirely to driving within a fraction of a second.

Divided attention does not always work while you are reading. Reading uses the visual and, for many people, the auditory sense. It limits conversation, inhibits other auditory activities like listening to the radio and prevents focusing on other visual activity because your eyes are focused on a page. One reason we find concentration while reading challenging is because it is so singly focused. As a result it can become tedious fairly quickly, especially if what is being read is uninteresting.

Reading and carrying out another activity at the same time is almost impossible. If only to demonstrate the point, it is worth an experiment.

## Experiment

1. Select a fairly light book to read and an audio book for you to listen to.
2. Put the audio book on fairly loud, then begin to read while it's playing.
3. Try to read and listen to the audio book at the same time.
4. After 5 minutes, stop reading and stop the audio book.
5. Write down everything you can remember from both the 'books'.
6. Count the number of words you read and check how fast you read. Then skim the book to check how accurately you remembered what you read.
7. Replay the audio book and check how accurately you remembered what you heard.

Try this out in several different situations: reading and listening to a conversation, reading and watching television, reading and having a conversation. Some combinations will be more difficult than others.

The purpose of this experiment is to notice what distracts your attention most. If you discover that you can read and complete another task at the same time, then you will have developed another skill that, if nothing else, will aid your time management.

Most importantly, enjoy the game.

### INTEREST AND MOTIVATION

The more you are interested in what you are doing, the easier it is to concentrate. Remember when you were last so engrossed in what you were doing that you lost track of time. Nothing distracted your attention. You were totally interested and motivated to reach a goal. There are three words here to take particular note of: **interested**, **motivated** and **goal**.

When you know what you are after (a goal) and why you are doing it (motivate), then the desire (interest) to complete the task successfully makes for total concentration.

If, however, the task is particularly boring and it is hard to find either motivation or interest, then the process is the challenge. You will need to make the decision, for example, that:

▶ *Your **goal** is to finish this task as quickly as possible.*
▶ *Your **motivation** is that you can get home sooner or get on with a more interesting task.*
▶ *Your **interest** is developing a system that will allow you to get through boring material faster and more effectively every time you are faced with it.*

There are two main ways in which concentration can be interrupted: by internal distractions and external distractions. In Chapter 8, Distractions and solutions, we shall discuss external distractions in detail. Here, we will look at internal distractions and how to reduce stress – one of the greatest contributory factors to lack of concentration.

## Stress and memory

### Remember this

Access to mass information can be stressful; dealing with mass information by using powerful choosing and reading strategies reduces stress. Very often the problem is not how much we have to get through, but the means we have at our disposal to do it.

One of the biggest destroyers of memory is stress. When you're stressed you release high levels of cortisol into your bloodstream. Cortisol is a hormone that affects you in a number of ways, depending on the amount released into your body at any one time. Cortisol destroys glucose, your brain's source of food.

If you have ever been in an accident or witnessed something traumatic you may have got through the experience, wholly or partly aware of it, but be unable to remember anything about the incident afterwards. Biologically speaking, you would have experienced an enormous amount of stress, and your body would have released large quantities of cortisol that went straight to your hippocampus and destroyed the glucose. With reduced food your brain did not have what was necessary to lay the memory down correctly, so although you saw everything – and maybe even spoke to people and walked around – the memories were not laid down in any form that can be recalled or they were distorted or encoded in what is known as 'state-dependent memory'.

**Insight**

State-dependent memory occurs when you remember something in a particular state and can only recall it when you are in a similar state. It's a challenge some people face when sitting exams in a tense, stuffy hall after studying in the relaxed comfort of their home.

Another, and less extreme, instance occurs when you are under a moderate amount of stress. If you are about to give a speech, meet a large group of people or introduce your partner to your boss for the first time, you may feel a slight fuzziness in your brain – you have all the details that you need for the occasion but you can't quite get the ideas, names or words straight.

Some medical experts believe that cortisol can affect your brain chronically and do more subtle damage in the long term. Because of the level of stress in most of our lives we have a constant drip of cortisol into our bodies. This cortisol goes round our system and into our brains, destroys glucose and turns calcium into free radicals that destroy brain cells from the inside out. This can cause age-related memory loss. People between 40 and 50 years old may feel that they are not thinking as fast and clearly as they did before. If this situation is left unchecked, it could have serious consequences.

No matter what age you are, if you take care of your body and mind by taking regular exercise, eating healthily, exercising your mind, relaxing and enjoying life, your memory will become more clear, more creative, more active and more accurate.

Those who adapt their lifestyle will find very little will happen that they notice overnight, but constant and determined action will be rewarded. There is no magic pill that can be taken for instant memory – if one were put on the market you should approach it warily or even avoid it. You have the natural capacity to be brilliant if you choose. All it takes is a little effort, common sense and the knowledge and belief that you have what it takes.

### REACTING TO STRESS

Stress arises when your situation outweighs your perceived ability to deal with it. Perception of your ability will vary day to day, moment to moment. 'Perception' is the operative word here. You may have no more to do on Tuesday than you had on Monday but because your mood or your environment is different, what you have to do may seem more than it really is. The perception that you cannot cope will increase, regardless of the reality of your current surroundings.

## Insight

Imagine two people walking down a street. Both of them see a bus narrowly missing a cyclist, or a child crying. When they reach the end of the street, one is tense and frustrated and the other shrugs and says, 'That's life.' Your reality is what you perceive.

There are a number of stressors that may affect your concentration:

▶ *Environment – Noise, chaos and pollution.*
▶ *Social – People, deadlines, financial problems.*
▶ *Physiological – Aches, pains, poor nutrition,*
   *lack of exercise.*

In some situations we respond to our natural instincts and run
from stressful situations. Most stress comes from situations we
cannot run from or fight with, instead we have to sit still and smile
while we boil inside. This is when damage may occur and this
is what we have to deal with if we are to concentrate fully and
effectively.

---

## Tips for improving your concentration

The following are different ways of dealing with and reinterpreting
stressful situations and improving your concentration.

### BREAK THE ROUTINE

If you were able to do only one thing to improve your
concentration, then breaking your routine should be the choice.
Taking a break will improve your memory, concentration, mood
and ability and enable you to continue for much longer than you
could without one. A break from what you are doing will give
you the opportunity to reassess your task, think of new ideas and
approaches and will ultimately help you to be more productive and
reduce your stress levels.

Your body is hormone driven and works on a cycle throughout
the day. When you feel that you need a cup of tea or coffee or you
start yawning or making mistakes your body is telling you it is time
to stop and rest. Listen to your body, but don't take the coffee (see
Chris Fenn's book *The Energy Advantage*). The longer you put a
break off, the more difficult it will be to get back to work after you
finally decide to take one. If you have a lot to do it is better to take

plenty of little breaks and have small snacks rather than working through the whole morning and stopping for a full lunch. If you do that you may have more concentration problems than you normally do in the afternoon.

### CARROT OR STICK

One way to encourage yourself to increase your concentration is to make sure that you reward yourself well. If you work in a conventional environment you may not feel that you are fully recognized or rewarded for your efforts. Instead of waiting for a reward for your work to come from somewhere else, take the responsibility of giving yourself a reward. At the beginning of the day determine what you are going to accomplish and what your reward to yourself will be. Vary your rewards. Make them things that are good for you and things that you really want – anything ranging from an evening at the theatre or in a steam room to a proper holiday for finishing a big project on time. If you find reading a chore this kind of incentive is especially useful. Make sure you have plenty of reasons to treat yourself. You will feel happier, your motivation will increase and your stress levels will reduce.

### RID YOURSELF OF CLUTTER

One environment you can control is your desk. A single piece of paper on your desk may attract your attention several times a day. If each piece of paper has a deadline attached to it, you will have a desk full of alarm clocks going off every five minutes, alerting you to the pressure you are under, interrupting your concentration, inducing chronic stress and causing long-term damage to your capacity to concentrate.

If you have a clear desk, your environment will look and feel under control. You may have a great deal to do but you will be able to tackle the tasks one at a time with a clear mind. The perception that your environment is out of control will diminish if it looks organized.

### MUSIC AS AN AID TO CONCENTRATION

Sounds that surround you can either make or break your working
environment. Have you ever been in an office and found the silence so
uncomfortable that you felt you must whisper even though you knew
you didn't have to? On the other hand, have you ever entered a room
so full of music and noise that you felt within moments that you had
to leave? These are extremes; there is a great deal of variation between
them. Our response varies as well; a song might come on the radio
one day and without hesitation we switch it off; on another occasion
we feel the urge to turn it up to full blast and sing along.

Music is a phenomenally powerful force – so much so that at one time in
China certain chords and sounds were banned by the rulers of the time
because they feared the effect the sound had on the population (from
*The Secret Power of Music* by David Tame, Turnstone Press, 1984).

For the purposes of this book we shall look only at music that will
help your levels of concentration. Listed below are a few pieces of
music that have been tested and proved to aid concentration and
learning. These particular pieces will enable you to relax physically
but remain mentally alert.

The important thing about music is that you should enjoy and
appreciate what is playing. If you play music you don't like while
you try to concentrate, all you will achieve will be agitation and
increased stress.

The music you select should have certain properties:

▶ *The music should be relatively gentle but not so gentle that it
  puts you to sleep.*
▶ *The music should have no words.*

> ▶ *The volume should be fairly low and unobtrusive.*
> ▶ *There should be plenty of variety.*

**Some suggestions**
- ▶ *Bach – Largo from Harpsichord Concerto in F Minor*
- ▶ *Corelli – Largo from Concerto Number 7 in D Minor, Opus 5*
- ▶ *Vivaldi – Largo from Concerto in D Major for Guitar and Strings*

## Insight

On the other hand, I'm reviewing this chapter in a café in Aberdeen and there's a mixture between Take That and Amy Winehouse playing in the background. The hum and hustle of the place is perfect for me. Find what works and stick to it.

### BRAIN FOOD – EATING FOR MAXIMUM CONCENTRATION

Every cell and molecule in your body changes and develops according to what you put into it. This includes the air you breathe, the liquid you drink and especially the food you eat.

If you have to concentrate for an extended period of time, the ideal eating pattern to follow is little and often – of the right stuff. In our fast-food society we tend to pick up what we can on the run. Snacks often include high-sugar foods that reduce our energy levels.

## Keep this in mind

In Chapter 5, Memory, a number of passages to allow you to practise different memory techniques have been included. They are about food and energy. Pay particular attention to them and make sure that the memory techniques you use work on them because they contain useful information.

## Exercises to increase and improve concentration

There is no one thing you can do to suddenly make concentrating in any environment easy. Concentration has to be developed and improved. Here are some exercises you can use to increase concentration and decrease stress.

### BREATHING

Although most of your brain cells would die within 3–5 minutes without oxygen, you can live a whole lifetime without breathing properly and not be fully aware of the consequences. Your body uses your breathing as a signal to tell you when something is wrong. When you are feeling stressed or threatened you notice it first in your breathing; when you are feeling tired you yawn to take in more air; when you are in a room with poor ventilation it is not long before you feel uneasy, get a headache or feel tired. These signals should not be ignored.

Correct breathing relieves a number of complaints, including stiffness, tension, irritability, headaches, fatigue and depression. Good breathing habits contribute considerably to your ability to concentrate and to reducing your stress levels.

There are several breathing exercises that don't take long to do and that you can do in any environment, all of which will help you increase and maintain concentration. These exercises are quick to learn. Practise them for a few minutes every day.

A good habit to develop is to practise a breathing exercise before you begin a reading session:

- ▶ *Select one of the exercises outlined below.*
- ▶ *Sit for a moment and relax.*
- ▶ *Practise the breathing exercise selected.*
- ▶ *State what you want to achieve and what your purpose is.*
- ▶ *Begin reading.*

This routine will take only a few moments and your body will very soon relax naturally when you settle down to read, increasing your concentration and decreasing tension.

### Discreet breathing exercise

If you are in a situation where it can't be obvious that you are carrying out a breathing exercise:

▶ *Take a slow, deep breath.*
▶ *Hold it for the count of 8 and slowly exhale.*
▶ *At each in-breath make sure you are breathing into your abdomen rather than your chest. To check this you would normally place your hands on your abdomen and find out whether it is moving or not. When you are in too public a situation to do this, focus your awareness on your waist – as you breathe you should feel a tightening of your clothing.*
▶ *Take three or four breaths like this and then relax.*
▶ *Accompany the breathing with a good stretch if you can.*

### Insight

Sometimes you feel as if only a good stretch will clear your head. Get some energy by moving, stand up for a while and stretch. Better still, go for a walk. Get out for a bit. Have a mini-adventure. It works every time.

### Quick breathing exercise

If you have only a few minutes, this yoga breathing exercise is wonderful for relaxing and focusing. It is especially good if you have been rushing, and have a time limit to stick to:

▶ *Close your eyes for a few moments.*
▶ *Place your right thumb on your right nostril and block it.*
▶ *Breathe in deeply and slowly through your left nostril for 6 seconds.*
▶ *Block both nostrils and hold for 6 seconds.*
▶ *Unblock your left nostril only and slowly exhale.*
▶ *Pause for 6 seconds.*

▶ *Then continue by breathing in through your right nostril,*
*closing both, and exhaling through your right nostril.*
▶ *Continue to do this for as long as you feel comfortable.*

## Stimulating alertness

If you are becoming tired and you still have much to do,
the following exercise will help increase your alertness and
wake you up. You can do this exercise in public.

▶ *Stand or sit up straight.*
▶ *Breathe in completely and naturally (into your abdomen).*
▶ *Hold your breath for a count of 6.*
▶ *Purse your lips and blow out short bursts of air fairly*
*forcefully until you have totally exhaled.*
▶ *Breathe in deeply again and repeat the exercise several times.*

## If that doesn't work ...

If breathing exercises don't work for you, don't push at
them. When you feel you need to relax a bit, just sit back
and close your eyes for several moments.

## Insight

Look after yourself – no matter how unorthodox your solution;
hiding in the loo, going for a walk, catnapping on your office
floor for 20 minutes. Listen to your body and your brain; a loss
of concentration or discomfort is usually a signal to take a break.

### BEING PRESENT AND IN PERSPECTIVE

A wandering mind is a symptom of lack of attention and low
concentration. Being present doesn't always come naturally. It is
easy for your mind to wander off to foreign lands and times. The
only way to learn how to remain present is to become aware of
when you are not present. Here is an exercise you can do in public
or in private. It is very relaxing and very effective.

- *Sit or stand still for a moment.*
- *First, close your eyes if you can and notice what you can hear. How many conversations can you make out? What are people saying? Can you hear any traffic? What is the furthest sound you can hear? What is the closest sound you can hear? What is the most familiar or the most foreign or unusual sound? What is the most or least pleasant sound? Identify every sound you can hear.*
- *Next, notice what you can feel. How close are people to you? What does the floor beneath your feet feel like? What do your clothes feel like on you? Is there a breeze? If so, what direction is it coming from?*
- *With your eyes open now, notice the colours. How many different shades of red or blue or orange can you see? What is the most common colour in your view? What is the least common colour in your view? Now notice the shapes you can see. If you observed your surroundings and had to describe them in terms of shapes only, and not what the objects really are, how would you describe them?*
- *Finally, appreciate your surroundings.*

You may notice that, no matter how noisy or chaotic your surroundings might at first seem, when you really pay attention and become present you are surprised at the level of comfort and relaxation you generate. This could simply be the result of knowing your surroundings for what they are instead of making interpretations of them.

Do this exercise often, especially when you are feeling that your environment seems to be getting out of control.

### DELIBERATE ACTION

This exercise will be useful if you have only a short piece to read and can't seem to focus your mind on it:

- *Carry out one of the breathing exercises, giving yourself time to sit still for a while and gather your thoughts first.*

▶ *Then, take the material you want to read and for 5 minutes read as slowly as you can without allowing your mind to wander. If you feel your mind is drifting, bring it back.*

▶ *If your mind drifts very much, read out loud for a short time. After a while your attention will focus. Your natural desire to get through the material and finish what you started will take over and your reading speed will increase.*

## MENTAL NUMBERS

You will be surprised how easily you can be distracted without realizing that it is happening. Try this simple experiment:

▶ *Count from 1 to 26. Notice at what number another thought comes into your head.*

Many people will have another thought in their minds by the time they reach 5. When you are counting it is easy to think of other things and still keep going because counting from 1 to 26 is a simple exercise. When you are reading, the mental energy needed to focus your attention increases and drifting thoughts can contribute to a lack of concentration.

You might like to use the following experiment to increase your concentration:

▶ *Simultaneously count from 1 to 26 and go through the alphabet from A to Z: 1 – A – 2 – B – 3 – C – 4 – D – 5 – E and so on.*

▶ *Imagine the numbers as being on the right side of your brain and the letters on the left side.*

▶ *Then switch sides; imagine the numbers on the left side of your brain and the letters on the right.*

How fast can you go? How far can you go before you realize your attention has drifted? When you can go through the alphabet (and up to 26) fluently going forwards, try this backwards.

When you feel your concentration drifting, do one of the earlier exercises a few times. This can be quite meditative and relaxing.

## TIME OUT

The stress reaction prevents concentration and inhibits memory. When you feel you are reacting to a stressful situation:

▶ *Sit back for a moment and do nothing. Just breathe and relax.*
▶ *Take stock of what needs to be done.*
▶ *Be aware of the time you have available.*
▶ *Decide what course of action you are going to take.*
▶ *Prepare yourself.*
▶ *Act.*

Worrying about how you will do everything you have to do is a distraction in itself and achieves little.

# TEN THINGS TO REMEMBER

1 *Take breaks whenever you feel your concentration wandering.*

2 *Follow the breathing and relaxing exercises.*

3 *Know your goal and purpose and stay focused on it – especially if you start to lose concentration.*

4 *Manage your environment.*

5 *Be firm with people who demand your attention unnecessarily.*

6 *Develop a routine that includes rest and recovery in your reading and working.*

7 *Enjoy what you do – reward yourself often and generously.*

8 *Practise being present.*

9 *Consciously decide to focus on the reading you need to do. Make it a priority.*

10 *If you're really struggling, stop and come back to it later.*

# 5

Memory

In this chapter you will learn:
- *the memory process*
- *the different types of memory*
- *how memory works and when it doesn't*
- *techniques for remembering what you read*
- *how to involve your senses as you read*

Good concentration is the first step to a good memory. At the end of a paragraph, chapter or entire book, have you ever had to go back to the beginning because you could not remember what you read? No matter how fast your reading speed, unless you remember what you read you will have wasted your time.

> **Insight**
>
> Don't sacrifice memory for speed. Focus instead on reducing the amount of reading you have to do by applying the five-step system thoroughly. Then, even if you choose to read slowly (word at a time), you'll still be getting through it faster than before.

To remember information for a long time you must revise. Revision needs to be fast. It would be frustrating to find yourself spending as much time trying to revise and recall what you read as you did reading it in the first place.

In this chapter we look at the memory process, how it works and how to get the best from your memory while you read.

## Memory myths

There is a danger that modern living is overloading the human memory system. With mass communication growing, more being printed than ever before and the emphasis of success moving from physical strength to mental power, we have to develop skills that help us keep up – let alone get ahead. The main factor contributing to overload is not necessarily the amount of information we are faced with, but rather our attitude towards it.

Normally we only become aware of our memory when we forget something. This is a big issue in reading because most people find that remembering what they want from what they read is challenging. This is mainly because they are not using an appropriate retention and recall strategy.

There are some basic principles about memory that should be considered first:

▶ *Memory is not a stand-alone system. It relies on perception, attention and reasoning.*
▶ *Memory is not a system that is based on isolated facts. Everything you remember is interconnected to other pieces of information in your memory.*
▶ *Memory retrieval relies greatly on association. The more organized your memory is, the easier it will be to recall information.*
▶ *New information is not stored separately from old information. Old knowledge helps make sense of new information and vice versa, which is one reason why it is easier to read material you know something about.*
▶ *Memory is not only designed to store information; it is designed for use.*
▶ *We speak about memory as if it were an object. We describe ourselves as having a good, bad or average memory, like having good or bad lungs. Your memory is not a thing – at least, it is certainly not a single thing. It is a series of processes that are taking place in your brain, all the time.*

▶ *Your memory can be trained. It has been said that there are no good or bad memories, just trained or untrained. With very few exceptions, and barring organic damage, everyone is born with a memory that can be developed.*

The more you use your memory, the stronger it will become. Many of the problems people have with their memories as they age are due to lack of mental exercise, lack of physical exercise, poor nutrition, excessive stress and poor coping strategies.

The basic guideline for improving your memory and ability to concentrate is that what is good for the body is also good for the mind. Stress is a major factor in memory loss. (You may want to review the information about stress in Chapter 4, Concentration.)

## Short-term, intermediate and long-term memory

Almost all of us at some point feel that our memory is most effective in the short term. Sometimes, we go through phases or times of the day when we seem to be unable to retain or recall anything.

### SHORT-TERM MEMORY

This part of the memory system holds information for only a few seconds. If you did not have this facility, every piece of information you gained by sight, hearing, smell, touch or taste would be remembered and accessible. This would make gathering new information very difficult because of interference. If you want to remember what is in your short-term memory you have to pay attention to it and take action so that you remember it for a longer period of time.

### INTERMEDIATE MEMORY

This information is retained for a matter of hours. Have you ever done or noticed something, been interested in it and decided that you were going to remember it because it was interesting, only to find a few hours later that you could not quite remember what it was? This is the intermediate memory at work. Information that is necessary for the time being is stored in this process. As soon as it is no longer required, it is discarded. This is what happens when you forget people's names. You meet them once, they are remembered while you see them, but after the event you might not think about them for a while and when you meet them again you cannot remember their name. You might recall where you met them and what they were wearing because your visual memory is stronger than your auditory memory (more on this later), but you may well have forgotten their name.

### LONG-TERM MEMORY

This is the aim for most reading. Your short-term memory will retain information long enough for you to make sense of what you are reading, intermediate memory will retain information long enough for you to make sense of the chapter, but your long-term memory will help you remember and make sense of the whole book and use the information when you need it. Long-term memory requires revision and application.

Long-term memory works with short-term and intermediate memory. As you read you are relying on 'old' knowledge stored in your long-term memory to enable you to make links and associations with new information. All three systems are totally interlinked and gaps or weaknesses in any one of them will prevent the whole system from working effectively.

## How memory works

There are many models of how the memory system works. In its simplest terms, your memory is divided into three parts:

▶ **Acquisition** – *Absorbing information.*
▶ **Retention** – *Keeping information in your head.*
▶ **Retrieval** – *Getting information out again.*

The memory may become unavailable at any point. The trouble is, you only know it is unavailable when you try to retrieve something – perhaps when you are standing in front of a person whose name you have forgotten, trying to introduce them to someone else whose name you have also forgotten.

There are some basic memory rules to follow at each phase to help you remember.

### MEMORY ACQUISITION

1 *The first rule of acquisition is:* **Pay attention**. *Most of the time we forget something because we did not have the opportunity to remember it in the first place. Have you ever read the title of a book, only to realize two seconds later that you have forgotten it? The chances are that your attention was somewhere else. The same phenomenon occurs when you read the content. If you have internal talk going on inside your head, asking yourself whether you are likely to remember what you are reading or not, you will probably not remember much at all.*

## Insight

This goes for remembering people's names as well; we hear but we don't listen and, three seconds later, we don't remember what they said. PAY ATTENTION! Be present. In fact, paying attention and being present are the best ways to make sure you remember anything.

2 *The second rule of acquisition is:* **Plan**. *Before you begin, think of when you are likely to use the information you are reading. Then, decide which memory tool (discussed later in the chapter) will help best when the time comes to use the information in the future.*

3 *The third rule of acquisition is:* **Be interested**. *Even if the material seems dull, find something in it that interests you. If you are bored, then parts of your brain will go to sleep and make paying attention even more difficult.*

**4** *The final rule of acquisition is:* **Be active.** *Read actively. Think about what you read. When you follow the five-step system and you prepare to read, spend some time thinking about what you already know on the subject. As we saw at the beginning of this chapter, your memory does not work in isolation. The more connections you make between new and old information, the easier it will be to understand what you are reading. Understanding is the key to remembering.*

## MEMORY RETENTION

Keeping information in your head is one thing; keeping it there in such a way that you can retrieve it later is a different matter.

Your memory thrives on association and order. The better organized your memory is, the easier it will be to retrieve information when you need it. You do not have to keep everything in your head. You can be just as organized on paper, so that you will know where to find information when you need it. The simple memory tools outlined in the next section will help you organize your reading so that retrieval is easy.

Rehearsal and revision are needed before information can be effectively retained in the memory. There are several ways you can achieve this. The least effective is rote rehearsal. Unfortunately, most of us used this method through school when we attempted to memorize text for exams or tests. This is ineffective because as soon as the memory is interfered with in any way the information disappears. For instance, when someone gives you a telephone number and then asks you where you put the keys, you will probably forget the telephone number since the fact that you have lost the keys will take your mind in several different directions. Memory interference and forgetting will be discussed later in this chapter.

The more time you have to think about, understand and work at what you are trying to remember, the better the chance you will have of remembering it.

One reason why we have difficulty retrieving information is that the retrieval method used is inappropriate. Memories are stored in several parts of our brain. When we try to remember what our front door looks like, several areas of our brain will be activated. We might:

▶ **See** *an internal picture of the door (visual).*
▶ **Hear** *the sound of it closing (auditory).*
▶ **Recall** *the last time we walked through it (kinaesthetic and proprioceptive).*
▶ **Remember** *the feeling of the last time we locked ourselves out (emotional).*
▶ **Smell** *the fresh coat of paint when we painted it last (olfactory).*

When we try to retrieve information, we often use only one access point. If you can re-create the whole experience as you remembered it, it will be easier for you to recall more information.

There are different types of memory retrieval, depending on how the information is presented to you. The easiest information to remember is information you can recognize. The multiple-choice section in an exam may be easier than questions where you have to provide the answer. Recognizing someone's face is often easier than remembering their name. You might notice that sometimes when you are looking for information you know you have read before, you might know where it is; you can see it on the page and when you find the page you recognize the text, although you cannot recall the information itself.

## Insight

This book is on reading, not memory. Go to your local bookstore and glance through books on memory development. Some of the techniques for remembering names, numbers, places or events seem a little odd but as soon as you try them you'll see that they work.

## Techniques for remembering what you read

There are many ways to remember what you read. Some are listed below. The aim is to be comfortable with all of them and be able to use the right one for the material you are reading. Everyone is different, so experiment with all the approaches.

### LINEAR

Make notes as you read or after each section. These should include your own thoughts, ideas and cross-references. The more you include your own ideas, the stronger your long-term memory will be.

### KEY WORDS

Highlight the words that carry the message. If you do make notes separately, ensure the key words are correct – you do not want a list of words that make no sense to you when you review the information in the future.

## Insight

Be careful not to overdo it. Try to stick to highlighting only a few words per sentence and perhaps only one key sentence per paragraph. If you highlight everything, you will end up with the same text, but underlined, coloured, circled and therefore more difficult to read.

### MARGIN READING

Many people are brought up to believe that books are to be kept in perfect condition. Unless a book is being presented as a priceless antique, it is a form of communication from the author to the reader. You start to take ownership of a book by writing in it or marking it. As well as underlining, circling and highlighting essential areas, you can note your opinions, whether you agree or disagree with what is written and mark what you do or don't understand. Then you can do something about that 'not understanding'. This should only be done if the book belongs to you, of course.

## Insight

Margin reading (and reading with a pen or pencil in your hand) will keep your eyes moving fast, your concentration on the page and your interest high because you'll be thinking about what you're reading instead of just reading the author's words.

### CONTEXT-MAPPING

This technique is based on questions and answers. As you go through the text, look for the answers to the when, what, where, who, why and how questions. Write the answers on an index card or on the text itself. You will often discover that you have all the information you need when you reach the end of it. In order to recall the information later, all you have to do is ask the questions again and the answers will be triggered.

### MIND-MAPPING

This is another way to make notes:

▶ *Write the key idea in the centre of a horizontal (landscape) page.*
▶ *The main ideas form thick branches from the centre.*
▶ *Secondary ideas flow from the main ideas.*
▶ *Tertiary ideas flow from the secondary ideas.*
▶ *Continue until you reach the finest relevant detail.*
▶ *Use as many colours as possible (with some material you will need five at least), and use symbols or pictures instead of words as far as possible.*
▶ *Use one word or idea per line.*

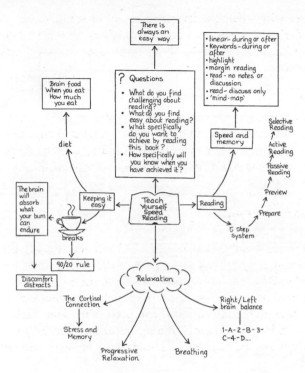

*hand-drawn mind-map*

## INDEXING

This technique is good for research:

▶ *Draw a line down the middle of a number of A5 cards.*
▶ *Write 'concept' on the left and 'definition' on the right.*
▶ *As you read and you come across the key concepts, write a few key words that summarize the concepts or ideas and in the other column note down any terminology (with definitions) that is new to you.*
▶ *File the cards under subject headings. When you read another book on the same subject, use the same cards and*

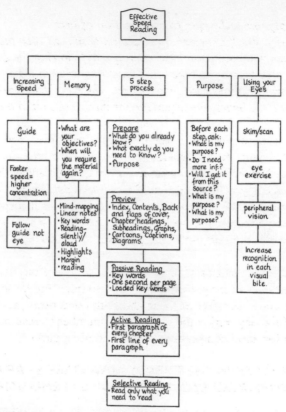

hand-drawn process-map of same information

add to and expand on the information you have already gathered.

## TESTING MEMORY TECHNIQUES

Four pieces of text follow. Each is approximately 500 words long. Read each as fast as you can for good comprehension, using any of the techniques outlined above.

▶ *Avoid using a memory strategy you are already familiar with; you already know how well that works or otherwise.*

- ▶ *Apply one technique to each section of text.*
- ▶ *Give yourself a maximum of 1 minute to read each piece of text.*
- ▶ *When you have completed reading and following the guidelines for each technique, take some time to write as much as you can remember about each piece of text. The more details you can recall, the better. Once you are satisfied, move on to the next one.*

The most important part of any memory technique is to make sure that you arrange the knowledge you are gathering into an order that suits you. The author will structure information in a way that makes sense to them; you have a different level of knowledge and a different background. Make sure that the new information is incorporated into what you already know and is arranged in such a way that later on, when you want to use it, it still makes sense to you.

The following sections of text have been very carefully selected. They give you an insight into the body rhythms and cycles that have an immense effect on your ability to concentrate at different times of the day. Enjoy the exercise. Remember to read as fast as you can for good comprehension, and to use a pacer.

**EXTRACT FROM THE ENERGY ADVANTAGE BY DR CHRIS FENN (PRINTED WITH THE AUTHOR'S PERMISSION)**

## Text 1

### SYNCHRONIZE YOUR BIOLOGICAL RHYTHMS

It's a familiar pattern. There are times during the day when you are firing on all cylinders – feeling particularly alive and focused, coping well with your work and shining at business meetings, or somehow coping with the demands of small children that would otherwise leave you frazzled. Yet there are other times in the same day – when you find yourself making simple inexplicable errors, and unable to concentrate or think clearly. The period of fatigue and

*(Contd)*

yawning that can descend around mid-afternoon is a common occurrence, but a couple of hours later we seem to have pepped up again and found a second wind. Most people believe that this spaced-out feeling results from the large meal they had for lunch. This is true to some extent – a full stomach does cause a diversion of blood supply to the intestine, which cuts back on the flow to the brain. But have you ever noticed that you don't get quite the same effect after a large breakfast? The mid-afternoon lethargy also occurs if you only have a small snack for lunch. So what's going on? What we eat is only partly to blame for the change in our mood and energy levels throughout the day; our mind and body activities are also ruled by natural cycles and rhythms.

## *TUNE IN TO YOUR BIOLOGICAL CLOCK*

Since the beginning of time, civilisations have set their routines and pace of life by the external cycles of the Sun and Moon. Only recently have we realised that we have our own internal clocks which also play a vital role in our everyday lives. Our bodies follow a pre-programmed sequence so that the essential functions of sleep, wakefulness, growth, repair and metabolism occur during the most appropriate times of day or night.

You may be familiar with the term circadian rhythm which refers to the biological cycle that occurs over 24 hours. Originally it was thought that our circadian rhythm was simply a daily alternation between being awake and asleep, but research now shows that there are other rhythms which have a powerful effect on how we feel and how efficiently we perform throughout the day. So, to maximise your everyday performance, you should tune in to your internal clock!

The exact site of the body clock in humans has yet to be determined, but in rats and other mammals it is located in two small groups of cells, one on either side of the brain, called the suprachiasmatic nuclei (SCN). The siting of the clock in this area is significant because the cells are part of a larger area known as the hypothalamus, a region of the brain that also controls body temperature, food and water intake, hormone secretion and sexual drive. When the SCN were removed, it was found that the rats' cycles of feeding, drinking and sexual activity were destroyed.

## Text 2

### *TUNE IN TO YOUR BIOLOGICAL CLOCK (CONTINUED)*

Wherever the clock is located in our bodies, there is no doubt that it is a sophisticated device, 'ticking' away and controlling what we feel – and when we feel it. The sleep/wake cycle is one of the body's most powerful rhythms that makes us feel alert during the day and sleepy at night. However, a British study carried out at Manchester University suggests that our cycle does not exactly coincide with the planet's 24-hour day. Kept in a room with continuous artificial light, and none of the daily external cues as a guide, the bodies of the Manchester test group adjusted to a 25-hour cycle.

This happens to many of us at weekends. Without alarm clocks, deadlines and appointments, staying up late on Friday or spending half of Sunday in bed, our rhythms free-run into the natural 25-hour cycle. People who are particularly sensitive find themselves feeling sluggish with the 'Monday morning blues' as they report to work slightly 'jet-lagged'. People suffering from blindness caused by retinal disease often lose synchrony with their family, friends and colleagues as their daily rhythm free-runs on a 25-hour cycle.

Research has shown that there are distinct variations, ruled by the circadian rhythms, in our physical and mental abilities. This is because during each complete cycle, body temperature, urine production, levels of glucose, cholesterol and other substances all rise and

*(Contd)*

fall; our mood, mind and body are constantly changing throughout the day and night.

Putting it all together – a typical day would begin around 7 a.m. Having sunk to its lowest point some time between 4 a.m. and 6 a.m., our body temperature begins to rise rapidly. This affects our metabolism, which also starts to speed up because enzymes (controlling various chemical processes in the body) work faster when the temperature is higher. These in turn kick-start the release of the rousing hormone cortisol, and we reach our peak mental performance some time between 7 a.m. and 12 noon. This is the best time for tackling problems – the boss or an important piece of work. After midday is not a good time for making decisions. Our body temperature starts to cool off again, levels of adrenaline and other hormones decrease, and mental ability generally gets put on the back-burner. This is when most people feel lethargic and notice a definite drop in efficiency.

People who work in Mediterranean countries have the right idea when they break off and have a siesta. It happens to coincide with the hottest part of the day – but it makes sense to synchronise with your body-cycles rather than fighting against them. After 3 p.m. our mental ability begins to pick up again and we can work well. From 4 p.m. to 7 p.m. we are at our physical peak, thanks to a rise in levels of the hormones noradrenalin and adrenaline (the new names for these are norepinephrine and epinephrine). These affect optimal nerve functioning and muscle co-ordination which helps manual workers to perform well, but this is the time to challenge for a game of squash or engage in some form of exercise. From 7 p.m. onwards, the body cools down along with the metabolic rate and levels of various hormones until we are back to our lowest ebb at 3 a.m. With this knowledge it is possible to schedule important business meetings or conference calls to take advantage of these peaks. As well as circadian rhythms, there are other cycles which may have a more immediate effect on our mood and overall health.

### *FORGET THE FAKE FATS*

In between indulging in the so-called forbidden foods, many of us go on the diet treadmill, which, until recently, meant eating as a penance cardboard-like fat-free foods. A few years ago, like low-calorie manna from heaven, came the fake fat revolution. These fake fats are substances (some are synthesised from sugars or proteins) that can provide the creamy mouth-feel of fats but without other Calories. Suddenly the supermarket shelves held no fears and there were no more forbidden foods. Chocolate, cream cakes, biscuits, gateaux, ice cream, custards and puddings now came without the fat. The theory is that these foods would replace the greasy, Calorie-laden alternatives and we could indulge in all this guilt free goodness and keep the bathroom scales in check. The reality is that it hasn't worked out like this. The food industry has been expanding on the profits from the low-fat revolution – but unfortunately so have we. According to UK government statistics, 16 per cent of women and 13 per cent of men are now obese – double the incidence five years ago – whilst almost half the population is overweight.

In the last five years, the average UK dress size for women has increased from 14 to 16. The food industry has done an excellent job in brain-washing us to accept just one message; fat is bad. As a result we have ditched every other health or nutritional consideration in pursuit of the belief that anything 'low fat' makes us thin and that fake fats are somehow 'healthy' foods. The food industry feeds this belief by spending a fortune on the research and development of an ever increasing number of synthetic fats and fat substitutes with which to produce new foods and add to the ever expanding range of fat free delights.

*(Contd)*

The latest and potentially most damaging of the fake fats is called Olestra. It is made from vegetable oil and sugar, but the molecules are too large and tightly packed to be absorbed by the body, so it passes straight through. Whilst other fake fats can't be heated beyond a certain point before breaking down, Olestra can be used in frying, making foods as greasy as you like but with the reassuring knowledge that fat will pass straight through your body. Olestra has recently been approved for use only in snack foods in America (although it may soon be permitted for a range of other fried foods and a cooking oil for home use). This approval occurred despite a blaze of controversy and opposition from health professionals, but is yet to be sanctioned by the UK Ministry of Agriculture Fisheries and Food. Why all the furore, you may ask.

Olestra's unique selling point is that it passes straight through your body, but when eaten in large quantities it causes what is charmingly described as 'anal leakage'. Individuals who have been trying Olestra have complained that it leaks, leading to stained underwear and an oily toilet. Nevertheless, the US Food and Drug Administration has allowed its use provided that Olestra-containing foods carry the government health warning 'Olestra may cause abdominal cramping and loose stools'. What is more, it takes with it the valuable fat-soluble vitamins A, D, E, and K as well as the carotenoids which play such a vital role in protecting the body against free radical damage.

## Text 4

### *FORGET FAKE FATS (CONTINUED)*

So, here we have a synthetic substance which, because it is not absorbed itself, inhibits the absorption of other nutrients which are flushed out of the body and down the toilet. What a crazy situation! Olestra and other fake fats should not be seen as the miracle cure for the growing obesity problem. Synthetic foods are deeply unfulfilling because they send the wrong signals to the brain. The messages to our appetite centre get garbled and confused when a food we associate with fat doesn't contain any. We lose touch with real hunger because the signals, released after eating, no longer guide and direct us towards making the best food choices. We end up eating 'mentally', relying on low-fat labels to guide us through the food maze. Studies have shown that the 'lite' and fat-free foods are so dissatisfying that we end up eating something to compensate. (The same is true of foods manufactured using artificial sweeteners. Some people become addicted to them in an effort to satisfy their need for sweetness. The solution lies not in another can of diet drink or sugar-free yoghurt, but to reach for real foods which are naturally sweet.)

Many of the foods containing fake fats are highly processed, requiring a cocktail of emulsifiers, stabilisers, thickeners and flavourings to replicate the mouth-feel and taste of the lost fat – which is another reason not to eat them. It is time to opt for a quality diet and not displace real foods with poor imitation of the genuine article.

The best way to control fat intake is to make the naturally low-fat (but nutrient-rich) foods such as fruits and vegetables, cereals, breads, pasta and rice the cornerstone of your eating habits. Then add in and enjoy smaller amounts of foods which are high in fat but provide as many of those omega-3 fatty acids as possible. Finally, if you enjoy foods with saturated fats, there is no need to eliminate them from your diet – or worse, feel guilty when you do eat them. Simply choose the best. Why settle for a chemically sweetened reduced fat chocolate bar which tastes so artificial when you can relish real, top quality Belgian or Swiss chocolate? Chewing on

(Contd)

rubberised, half-fat cheese is an insult to your taste buds compared with enjoying a really excellent, but small piece of your favourite – and the finest – Cheddar, Stilton, Brie or Parmesan. We should be taking care over our food, like the Italians and French, cooking it with love, appreciating its quality and eating it for its flavour!

Now answer the following questions:

▶ *How did you do?*
▶ *What difference did you find in effectiveness of the techniques?*
▶ *Did you find that you were slipping back to old habits?*
▶ *Did any of the techniques slow your reading down?*

When selecting the best methods for remembering what you read, it is important to remember that everything you read is different and each type of reading material needs a different memory approach – depending on what your purpose is, how familiar you are with the information and how much time you have to read it.

It is most important that the techniques you select should facilitate good recall and high reading speeds. Practise and experiment with different types of text. Remember that the more involved you are with your reading the better your recall, understanding and comprehension will be. The way to do this is to read with more than just your eyes.

## Multi-sensory reading

Do you remember your front door? Do you remember what it sounds like when you close it? What does fresh paint smell like? What does it feel like to be locked out? What colour is it?

Multi-sensory reading uses as many of your senses as possible to help you make sense of and absorb information.

Here are some ideas on how to involve your other senses as you read:

▶ **Sight** – *Imagine what you are reading in your mind, create a film of the story you are being told.*
▶ **Hearing** – *Speak to people about the subject, ask questions as you read, teach someone else, make up rhymes and stories.*
▶ **Touch** – *Draw pictures and symbols representing the information. If the information is something you can do, do it instead of just reading about it.*

The more senses you involve in learning new information, the easier it will be to recall it because the information will be accessible via more than one function of your brain.

The five-step system and memory-support techniques work if you simply use them. The more you practise and the more you become aware of memory, the better you will become at speed reading.

### VISUAL AND AUDITORY MEMORY

Most people remember films far more accurately than books. Visual memory appears to be much stronger than auditory memory.

To activate your visual memory for what you read, use your imagination to picture what you are reading in as much detail as possible. This can be particularly challenging with non-fiction material, depending on what the subject is. The more you can picture what you read, the easier it will be to recall later on. Also, you will realize as you develop your visual memory that the picture becomes clearer as your understanding of the subject grows.

# Forgetting

Unsurprisingly, forgetting is the most frustrating part of reading. Your ability to concentrate and the memory technique you choose will help you remember what you read. But sometimes, forgetting happens in spite of them.

Our difficulties in retrieving information give us a very good idea of how our memories work. Memories are often available (we know we have read something, or seen it; we can remember where we were when we encountered it in the first place) but still they are not accessible (we just cannot quite remember it fully). This phenomenon is sometimes called 'on the tip of the tongue'. The long-term memory is organized in categories, much like a mind-map; one thing reminds you of the next and so on. If the links between the associations are broken, the information may become inaccessible or you may forget it entirely.

### *FACTORS CONTRIBUTING TO FORGETTING*

## Lack of attention
▶ *Problem* – *If you don't hear, see or notice something, you'll have no chance of remembering it.*
▶ *Solution* – *Increase your concentration. Chapter 4 provided you with a number of exercises and ideas on how you can do this. Chapter 9 will give you ideas on how to diminish distractions.*

## Interference
▶ *Problem* – *Interference can be retroactive or proactive. Retroactive interference comes from new information you are reading. If you think of telephone numbers, retroactive interference is involved when you cannot remember your old telephone number because your new one has taken over.*

*Proactive interference is when old information interferes with new information. Thinking of your telephone number again, this is involved when you cannot remember your new number because your old one keeps coming into your mind instead.*

▶ *Solution – The best way to work around retroactive and proactive interference is to rest between different pieces of work. This gives your mind time to consolidate new information, separate out old and perhaps integrate new information with current knowledge (unless it is your telephone number). After you have taken a break, revise the text to make sure that you have not confused old and new information.*

## Lack of interest or motivation

▶ *Problem – If you are neither interested nor motivated, remembering what you read will be almost impossible. Tiredness contributes to this. Even if you are working on something you are interested in, that interest will soon fade if you are tired.*

▶ *Solution – It is important to find something to motivate you, no matter how small or seemingly unrelated to the task it is. There must be something in it for you. And take breaks. Take them as often as you feel you need them, but for at least 10–15 minutes every hour to hour and a half.*

## Insufficient links or associations

▶ *Problem – If the subject is particularly new to you, making sense of the ideas may be difficult. If you cannot make sense of the ideas you will find it very difficult to remember.*

▶ *Solution – As you follow the five-step system you will be building a framework of knowledge. The bigger the framework becomes, the easier it will be to form links and associations for new knowledge. Spend as much time as you need on Step 2 (preview); this step allows you to build a structure for the material.*

## Insufficient revision

▸ **Problem** – *Memories are made of memory traces. They fade if they are not reinforced.*

▸ **Solution** – *A basic guideline is to revise seven times in ten days – or develop a very good filing system. To remember what you read in the long term, use the information. As mentioned under Memory myths, the memory process is designed for use, not just for storage.*

# TEN THINGS TO REMEMBER

1 *Memory is not a stand-alone system. It doesn't mean because you memorize something that you understand it.*

2 *The more you understand something the easier it will be to remember it.*

3 *Memories are linked by association. Make connections between new information and what you already know.*

4 *Use what you learn.*

5 *Train your memory. Don't use a bad memory as an excuse not to remember people, conversations, numbers or what you read.*

6 *Pay attention! If you don't hear or see or absorb the information in the first place you'll have no chance of recalling it when you need it.*

7 *Books are not sacred. Write in them (unless they're not yours or priceless antique). Normal books are to be interacted with. Underline, circle, highlight, scribble in them.*

8 *Use your imagination while you read.*

9 *Reinforce what you read by reading a number of books on the same subject.*

10 *Choose to remember. Don't assume that information will stick just because you have understood it the first time you've read it.*

# A book is a book is a book

In this chapter you will learn:
- *how to read different types of materials*
- *how to evaluate text by critical reading*

## Reading different types of material for different reasons

You've looked at the five-step reading system and considered speed reading and memory development. Now it's time to look at what you read and how to apply the different reading techniques to ensure you get the most out of them.

The way you approach a document (book, newspaper, memo or whatever) should be driven by your purpose. Why are you reading it? When will you use the information next?

### TECHNICAL MATERIAL

This type of reading may be fairly easy because most technical writing is well structured. Also, you rarely have to read and remember everything about the text without being able to refer to it later on when you need it. Apply the five-step system in its entirety for this type of reading and use a memory technique that works well for you. Try mind-maps. If you don't like mind-maps, try a process-map (see Chapter 5, p. 82). These techniques allow you to see how information, ideas and practices are linked and what effect they have on each other.

## NON-FICTION FOR LEISURE

This is perhaps the easiest of all non-fiction reading simply because you are already relaxed and interested in the subject (in the ideal positive learning state). Most non-fiction, like technical writing, is fairly well structured so the five-step system can be readily applied.

It is easy to become absorbed in 'work-related' reading and not put time aside for leisure reading and knowledge gathering. If you have a lot of work to do, you may feel uncomfortable or guilty about taking time out for leisure reading, albeit non-fiction. A good way to get around this is to make increasing your reading skill part of your purpose, with the intention of becoming able to read work material more effectively. If you only ever read text that is difficult or that bores you, your passion for reading will soon be subdued. Make time to read what you want to read.

### READING FOR RESEARCH

The good thing about reading for research is that your purpose is normally very clearly defined and you are looking for something quite specific. Apply the five-step system and follow the guidelines for reading for study in Chapter 10, Working and studying for a living. If you are studying and working at the same time Chapter 10 will give you ways of organizing all your reading from the start of the course to the end of the exam.

### READING FOR WORK

This section is particularly concerned with mail and memos. The rule here is: **Be selective.** The trouble with the reading you do for work is that there may be an activity attached to every document. Before you read anything – especially if it is long and you think it may take you a while or if it seems to land on your desk often – ask a few questions:

▶ *Who wants you to read it?*
▶ *Why do they want you to read it?*
▶ *What are you likely to have to do with the information as a result of reading?*

Once you have established that there are good reasons for reading documents take the following steps:

- ▶ **Decide how much time** *you will devote to reading in-coming mail or memos.*
- ▶ **Preview the documents** *with one thing in mind: can this go in the bin? Then sort them into two piles, one of which goes straight into the bin and the other requires further attention.*
- ▶ **Passive read or skim** *all of the documents in the further attention pile and ask one question of each: can this be filed or does it require action? Put the pile for filing aside ready to file.*
- ▶ **Actively read** *the remaining pile. Use Post-it notes or write the actions that are to be taken directly onto the document.*
- ▶ **Finally, plan the actions** *into your day or week. Then put the relevant documents into the appropriate file so that you can retrieve them easily when you need them.*

## Insight

Remember that most work-related writing is done by people determined to make themselves look good, not by people who consider how you like to read and what you really need to know. Don't feel bad about ditching the irrelevant bits!

### NEWSPAPERS

Note that this section does not apply to the casual, relaxed read of the Sunday morning paper unless you want it to.

Reading a newspaper should be approached with the same preparation as any other reading. The five-step system works very well for papers; however, it may not be necessary to use all five steps in order. You can read a paper very quickly by following three very simple steps:

1 **State your purpose** – *Are you reading to gain an overview of the whole paper or are you looking for a particular story?*
2 **Preview and passive read** *the entire paper by looking at the headlines and reading the first paragraph of any story*

*that looks interesting. Circle the articles you would like to return to.*

**3** **Actively read** *the selected articles for the information you want.*

To read newspapers effectively:

▶ *Set a time limit and stick to it.*
▶ *Read story continuations (often on other pages) as you come to them. This is a good indication of how much attention you pay to reading a paper. If you come to the second part of a story several pages later but cannot remember the details of the first part, take a break.*
▶ *Since most of the facts are normally in the first few paragraphs of a story, start reading each story you select fairly thoroughly at the beginning and then speed up and skim the rest, picking up information you identify as relevant.*
▶ *Ask yourself:*
  ▷ *What is the position of the paper with respect to political slant?*
  ▷ *Have you previously read articles by specific journalists before? Do you like their style or approach?*
  ▷ *Is this the best paper to read for your purpose?*

Unlike most other forms of writing, a newspaper story can be broken into parts quite easily. A narrative takes you from the beginning of a story to the end and if parts are missed out some of the meaning goes with it. A newspaper is not as unified as that. A story can be read with sections missed out of it – you may lose some detail but the story will remain the same. Very little interpretation can be made of most newspaper stories; they are real events involving real people – often given an editorial 'flavour', style or angle by the paper and the writer.

## MAGAZINES

Magazines (especially special interest or trade magazines) are slightly different from newspapers. A newspaper is one of many sources of news. If you miss anything from the paper, you will probably be able to get the story from the television, radio or Internet. Most magazines come out only once a month or once a quarter. A magazine should be treated like a short textbook. Follow all the steps of the five-step reading system to get the best out of it. If there is information in the magazine that you are likely to need again there are several things you can do to make it easily accessible:

▶ *Read the magazine with Post-it notes to hand. As you find articles you are interested in, note the page number and title and write a brief summary (just a sentence or two) on a Post-it note. Stick the note on the front of the magazine and file the magazine in a file dedicated to 'interesting articles'.*

▶ *If you don't want to keep the whole magazine, tear out the relevant pages or photocopy the articles you want, and file those away with a brief summary of what the article is about.*

▶ *Add why you thought the article might be useful to the Post-it Note. When you return to articles at a later date you will find it easier to place them in order of priority. Going through the file to see what you no longer require and can throw away will also be easier with this extra information on each.*

▶ *Be picky. Most magazine reading is for interest. You are unlikely to be tested on it but you may want to talk about it. Select the articles that interest you and think about how what you read fits into your existing knowledge.*

## NOVELS

The more you read, the faster you will become. Speed reading skills will give you the choice to read as slowly or as quickly as you like.

If you enjoy novels and you want to read more of them, you may find this strategy useful:

▶ *Preview the book thoroughly (excluding the actual story) – look at the front and back covers, read any author's notes, biography or foreword, take a good look at the author's photograph if there is one. Do you like the author's style? Do you like the look of the author? Does the back page blurb intrigue you? What you do at this point will shape your attitude towards the book. Your attitude will affect whether you are likely to enjoy the book or not.*

▶ *Next, read the first page. Does it grab your attention?*

▶ *If it does and the book passed your preview test, then read on and enjoy the book. If not, then skim the book picking up key words and reading the first few sentences of each chapter. If the book still doesn't catch your imagination, you can choose not to read it.*

▶ *If you do decide to read the novel but you don't have much time, then practise 'finding the story' (see below). This technique is for novels or very short pieces of text that don't require the full five-step treatment.*

▶ *If you get bored with the story half-way through the book, give yourself permission to put it down. If the storyteller does not keep you intrigued, you do not have to carry on.*

## Find the story...

As you read a novel, look only for the pieces of text that carry the story. Skim over the description. Most novels carry the story in conversation between the characters. As you read you will become familiar with the layout and be able to identify where the descriptive text starts and ends. If you begin to really enjoy the novel and want to read everything, you can change your technique and slow down a bit to enjoy the scenery.

### E-MAILS

E-mails are a blessing or a curse, depending on who sends them. Rule 1 with e-mails is to do to others as you want them to do to you. If you don't want huge letters and memos and masses of junk mail, don't send any of these unless absolutely necessary. If someone repeatedly sends you e-mails you don't want, whether they are jokes or longer stories, be firm and straightforward and ask them not to. Treat e-mails like traditional mail; if you know it is junk before you open it up, bin it.

A good way to screen your e-mails is to use the feature that allows you to have your inbox screen split. The top half has a list of all the messages and the bottom half lets you read the e-mail without actually opening it. This saves time. Some systems have a preview function which allows you to view only the first few words, which is also time-saving.

If there are attachments to an e-mail and you need to read them fast, it may be best to print them out. If you prefer to read from the screen, there are some ideas on how to do this without straining your eyes in Chapter 9, Real-world reading. There are also ideas on how to prevent eyestrain in Chapter 7, Your eyes and effective reading.

## INSTRUCTIONS

In reading instructions, planning is the key. Unlike most other reading, almost every word counts in instructions. Missing one or two may mean you never get to build what you set out to build. Also, most manufacturers write instructions in such a way that they are quick and easy to follow, but not necessarily quick and easy to understand. Remember that some instructions are translated from foreign languages and the translations may not be entirely clear or accurate.

Here are some tips on reading instructions:

▶ *Read through all the instructions before you do anything. Go from Step 1 to the end; don't miss anything out at all. If it looks a lot or seems that there is a lot involved in the activity, relax and gather all the information you need before doing anything else.*
▶ *The first time you read the instructions, mark off phases of the job so you break the task into manageable chunks that relate to how you want to manage your time when you do the job.*
▶ *If there are any pictures, study them thoroughly.*
▶ *Once you have read the instructions and have an idea of what the job entails, make sure you have everything you need.*
▶ *After you have gathered everything you need to do the job (tools, equipment, assistant perhaps), go through the*

*instructions again, this time focusing on each of the phases you identified in the first step.*

▶ *Do things one at a time. But while you are following one step keep the next one in mind so that you know where you are heading.*

▶ *As you go, tick off the steps as you finish them.*

▶ *If you come to a step you don't understand, think of something you did in the past that is similar to the job you are doing now. Look at any picture related to it and carry on unless you feel that carrying on will prove to be a disaster. If you think a disaster may be looming, stop. Contact the manufacturers or call someone to come and help.*

▶ *Reward yourself once you have finished.*

▶ *Following instructions is much like following a set of directions. When you can visualize the finished product or the destination, completing the task will be much easier.*

## If you still have problems with some pieces of specialist text

If you find some paragraphs confusing, mark them and carry on. If the meaning doesn't become clear as you read, go back to those sections and read them more carefully. Check other sources if you have to.

If, however, you become more confused as you read the text, you may have missed the key word or idea in the whole passage. If this happens:

▶ Stop
▶ Take a short break
▶ Reassess your purpose
▶ Follow the first four steps of the five-step system thoroughly.

Selective reading will be very slow and frustrating if you miss the point of the text.

## Critical reading

One of the purposes of reading critically is to evaluate the text. The aim is to evaluate the whole text or argument, finding out the author's intention and judging at the end whether they were successful. Here are a few guidelines for critical reading:

- ▶ *Read with an open mind.*
- ▶ *Know your own opinion before you begin so that you are not unduly swayed by the author's argument.*
- ▶ *Don't jump to conclusions.*
- ▶ *Keep asking questions.*

In order to read critically it is useful to understand critical language fully. In Chapter 11, Useful information and speed practice test, there is a list of critical language with space to add definitions (see p. xx).

Reading critically and effectively with an open mind involves the following:

- ▶ *Understand the literal meaning of the text. Be sure you understand how the names, dates, figures and facts all fit together.*
- ▶ *After that, look for the suggested meaning of words and phrases.*
- ▶ *Recognize the tone. Is the author being sarcastic, honest, factual or whimsical?*
- ▶ *Create an image in your mind of what the text is about and look for any gaps in the story.*
- ▶ *Look for any comparisons, metaphors, similes, clichés or other figures of speech.*
- ▶ *Once you have all the information you need, make a value judgement. Did the author succeed in what they set out to do? Are you convinced by their argument? If you are not, are you at least satisfied that although you don't agree with the author, the structure is sound? What would it take to convince you? If the author failed, why?*

Fiction and non-fiction are both open to critical evaluation. The following advice will help you, but it is most important to bear in mind that each category contains a huge range of different types of material and the questions suggested will not relate precisely to everything you read.

## Insight

Critical reading is a vital habit to develop. Most people are too easily suckered into believing something just because it's in print. This goes for everything in print; from newspapers to religious texts. Do yourself a favour and THINK while you read.

### EVALUATING NON-FICTION

Follow the six steps above and ask yourself additional questions:

▶ *What assumptions are being made by the author?*
▶ *What evidence does the author present?*
▶ *Is it convincing?*
▶ *Do any arguments about cause and effect really relate to each other?*
▶ *Is the conclusion logical?*
▶ *Is what the author writes more a matter of opinion than of research?*
▶ *Is the writing emotive?*
▶ *What conclusions can you draw?*

### EVALUATING FICTION

An evaluation of a fictional text is based mostly on how you feel about the text, not on fact or what you know about a subject. Fiction may contain factual information but differs from non-fiction in containing assumptions and lacking evidence.

Some questions to ask as you read fiction:

▶ *Is the story believable? Even if it is far-fetched and imaginative, can you believe it could happen?*

- ▶ *Are the characters and events believable? Do they have a purpose or do they seem to have no purpose other than get in the way of the story?*
- ▶ *Are conflicts justified or has the story succumbed to violence for its own sake?*
- ▶ *Are the characters superficial? Do you get to know them? Has the author developed them well?*
- ▶ *Does the story lead you or do you find yourself wondering where it is going?*
- ▶ *Does the plot flow?*
- ▶ *Are you gripped and intrigued?*
- ▶ *Do you find it easy to put down or not?*

Reading critically will give you the insight into the true value of the text. If you find there is none, save yourself time and put the book down.

# TEN THINGS TO REMEMBER

1 Not all reading material is the same. Treat everything you read based on what you need it for.

2 Take time to read what you want to read. Not just what you have to read.

3 When it comes to non-fiction (work-related) reading be selective. Knowing where to find information is often better than having it all stored in your head.

4 It's up to you to decide how much time you spend on reading incoming mail. Don't let it control your day.

5 Always ask if reading material (especially work-related) can go in the bin.

6 When catching up on world news, be curious. Take a minute to wonder what's going on behind the story.

7 Use the five-step system on newspapers and magazines.

8 Read instructions. Either that or let someone else build your latest IKEA acquisition.

9 Whenever you read the newspaper or a magazine or work-related material – read critically.

10 On the flip side to number 9, read with an open mind. You're not going to learn anything if all you look for are ideas that confirm your current beliefs. Consider the possibility that you might be wrong.

# Your eyes and effective reading

In this chapter you will learn:
- *speed reading basics*
- *how to read for understanding*
- *how to care for your eyes by using exercises and nutrition*
- *how to prevent and cure eyestrain*
- *how to read from a PC monitor*

Your most important reading tools are your eyes. Any discomfort or strain will affect concentration immediately. If you are tired or if the lighting is wrong, you are likely to experience discomfort in your eyes and a headache may follow quickly. Soon after the headache begins you will begin to lose concentration and reading will become difficult. It is easier to prevent problems with your eyes than it is to have to treat them when something goes wrong due to bad habits. Those who have recurring problems with eyestrain should consult an optician if they have not seen one recently. Some eye problems are linked with medical conditions; ask your doctor if you think there may be a connection between your eyesight and your general health.

The explanations and exercises in this chapter will give you an understanding of what your eyes do while you read.

## Speed reading basics

The main reason why most people have an average reading rate of 150–250 words per minute is that this is approximately the rate at which people speak.

As you read this paragraph, listen to what is going on inside your head. Do you hear a voice inside your head while you read? Are you saying the words in your mind? This happens because of the way most people are taught how to read.

When we are taught to read we learn to recognize one letter or sound at a time; then, when we have mastered that, we progress to recognizing one word at a time. The next step is being able to read out loud so that our teacher can see that we have learned to recognize the words accurately. Then we are left to read to ourselves.

That is how the inner reading voice becomes a habit. Instead of reading out loud we read silently. So when we talk about reading with our ears instead of our eyes, that is exactly what happens. You learn that you have to hear the words to understand what you are reading rather than understand them by seeing them.

When you read to yourself, you read in your head at the same rate as when you read out loud. At the beginning, reading to yourself is quite slow because you are still learning to recognize the words.

## Ears or eyes?

As long as you read by saying each word 'out loud' to yourself in your mind you will only be able to read as fast as you can speak. For most people this is between 150 and 250 words per minute.

You can only hear or say one thing at a time but you can see millions of things simultaneously. Learning to speed read involves learning to use one of the largest and most important sections of your brain, your visual system, more effectively.

Learning to read with your eyes instead of your ears will be the biggest step you take towards making a dramatic increase in your reading speed.

As you read more and go further into the education system your reading rate increases because your vocabulary increases. But your reading strategy does not change.

Reading is the slowest visual exercise we do. Look outside the nearest window for 3 seconds, then close your eyes and describe (by speaking) what you saw. How long did it take you to see what you saw and how long did it take you to say what you saw? Speaking to yourself when you read is the same as looking at a spectacular view or watching a film and, instead of visually understanding it, translating what you see into words that take several times longer to form, communicate and then be understood by someone else.

Visual memory and auditory memory are located in different parts of the brain. When you read slowly, giving yourself time to see every word and read with your ears, you are accessing the auditory, front-left portion of your brain. This is the least effective part for storing medium- or long-term memory.

When you first start to learn to read with your eyes instead of your ears, your comprehension will diminish initially because you are beginning to use your strong visual memory for something to which it is not accustomed. Your brain needs time to adjust to this new activity. This is perfectly normal. After a few hours of practice (in the beginning) and maybe 15 minutes a day for a few days you will find comprehension returning to what it was. Your memory will become longer term and more integrated than before. The process is similar to what happens, for example, when you learn to touch type instead of looking at the keyboard and typing with one finger.

## Reading for understanding

The aim of speed reading is to learn how to read more than one word at a time, and to do that you have to read with your eyes instead of your ears. Your comprehension will increase at the same time as your speed increases because when you read more than one word at a time you read phrases rather than isolated words. The meaning the author wants to put across is in the phrase, not the isolated word. Meaning is in groups of words so the more words you are able to comprehend at one time, the better your comprehension, understanding and subsequent recall will be. You will understand more because you are reading in terms of ideas, thoughts and images rather than isolated words that mean nothing by themselves.

An exercise later in this chapter (pp. 117–118) will help you increase your confidence in reading with your eyes instead of your ears.

## THE BIOLOGICAL CHALLENGE

Your eyes move very fast. They can process large amounts of information rapidly. If you read slowly your eyes will tend to wander. The pacer will go a long way towards preventing that. Remember the exercise you did in Chapter 2 (p. 27) that showed you how differently your eyes moved when they had something to follow? Go back and refresh your memory if you need to.

There are some eye movements you can do something about and some you can't:

1 **Fixation time** – *Your eyes need a certain amount of time to be able to absorb information. Try this experiment next time you are a passenger in a car. As you travel, keep your eyes fixed on one point, not letting them settle on anything flying by the window. Does your view become blurred? Next, as you go pick out certain parts of the landscape and follow them briefly. You might notice that what you look at becomes clear while the background is blurred. The same applies to reading. Your eyes need to rest – albeit briefly – on groups of words to be able to see them. The more words you can see and recognize in a single visual 'bite', the faster you will be able to read.*

2 **Peripheral vision** – *Try an experiment. Place your finger on the middle of the page and look at it. What else can you see? Where you are sitting? Perhaps the room you are in or*

*other surroundings? Your peripheral vision gives you the
ability to see an enormous amount in a single visual bite.
Now, without moving your eyes from the middle of the page,
try to read the words at the edges of the page.*
*How did you do?*
*You will find that although you could see the words, you
may not have been able to 'read them'. When you were taught
how to read you were taught to focus on one word at a time.
Being able to expand what you can recognize within your
peripheral vision takes practice. There are some exercises
later in this section that will help you increase peripheral
perception – you can do some of them while walking down the
street.*

3 **Regression and progression** – *These are visual tics. They are
a result of poor concentration and lack of confidence in your
memory.* **Regression** *refers to the habit of going back to previous
words or paragraphs to make sure you have understood them
or remembered them accurately.* **Progression** *refers to the habit
of jumping forwards for no particular reason.*

Studies of how people's eyes move when they read have been
done in the USA. Groups of people were given texts to read.
At the bottom of the test piece was the figure $3,000,000.00.
Before they had read half the page the eyes of all the readers
moved to the bottom of the text to see what the $3,000,000.00
was all about.

In terms of wasting time, several things happen when you do
this kind of thing:

▶ You forget what you have just read.
▶ Your comprehension drops because you are reading
something out of context.

Reading with a pacer and following the five-step system will enable
you to change your reading habits for the better. The following
exercises will help you.

Don't get fixated on getting rid of the voice in your head. Focus on the five steps, your purpose, memory and concentration, and one day the voice, if not totally gone, will have reduced to the degree that you only hear it when you read something technical or complicated.

## Did you know?

It is thought by some researchers that most eye problems are caused by lazy eye muscles and strain and that short-sightedness, long-sightedness, stigmatism and other visual complaints can be cured by a series of exercises. William Bates, a New York ophthalmologist, began to question how vision problems were diagnosed and treated and developed new ways of dealing with visual difficulties. He started by curing himself of presbyopia (far-sightedness). His work is well documented; some of the exercises he developed are included in this book and are very good for relieving eyestrain, which according to Bates is the primary cause of many eye problems.

### INCREASING YOUR SPAN OF RECOGNITION WITHIN YOUR PERIPHERAL VISION

When we learn to read we learn by recognizing individual parts of a word. This means that our reading is always fairly fragmented. If you can remember back to when you first learnt to read, you will recall that you had to break each word down to make sense of it, something like this:

1 2 3 4 5 6 7  8 9 10  11 12 13 14  15 16  17  18 19 20 21  22 23 24 25 26 27  28 29 30 31
R e a d i n g  o n e  w o r d  a t  a  t i m e  w a s t e s  t i m e
32 33 34  35 36 37 38 39 40 41 42 43 44  45 46 47 48 49 50 51 52 53 54 55 56 57  58 59 60
a n d  d i m i n i s h e s  c o n c e n t r a t i o n  a n d
61 62 63 64 65 66 67 68 69 70 71 72 73
u n d e r s t a n d i n g

Gradually you learnt how to string the letters together but you still only focused on one word at a time:

   1      2    3  4 5  6   7    8    9     10
Reading one word at  a time wastes time and diminishes
   11         12       13
concentration  and  understanding

The aim is to increase our visual span so that we can read more than one word at a time and increase our reading rate:

        1                             2
Reading one word at a time     wastes time and diminishes
        3
concentration and understanding

The larger the piece of text we can recognize in a single visual bite, the easier and more visual reading will become:

         1
Reading one word at a time wastes time
         2
and diminishes concentration and understanding

Ultimately, our aim is to be able to read more than one line at a time.

         1
Reading one word at a time wastes time
and diminishes concentration and understanding

An exercise to develop this skill can be found on pages xx–xx.

## Exercise directions

In the pyramid of numbers and letters in Exercise 1 below, focus on the hash marks (#) down the centre of the pyramid. The aim is to see how much you can read with your peripheral perception. Write down what you can see. Don't move your eyes from the centre of the row. Although you will be tempted to focus on the end of the row, you must try to keep your eye on the centre hash for the purpose of the exercise. You may notice several things:

▶ You may not be able to see some of the letters and numbers on the longer lines. This is normal. There is a point where your optic nerve enters your eye, creating a blind spot.

▶ If your eyes are of equal strength you may find that you can see more to the right of centre than you can to the left. This is because we read from left to right and our eyes are conditioned to look in that direction for new text. If you were brought up reading Arabic or Hebrew you would probably find that you could see more to the left instead of the right of centre.

**Exercise 1**

Place your pacer on the first hash and move it down the centre of the pyramid. Keep your eye on the hash marks in the centre. What can you see on either side of the hash marks without moving your eyes away from the centre?

S # p
2 E # 7 e
d R 8 # E 5 a
D 2 5 I 3 # n G 5 8 y
6 B 2 9 0 6 3 # R 8 3 4 2 N l
3 9 g 9 2 E 5 4 n # 8 5 2 i 4 u S 7 p

## Exercise 2

Follow the instructions for Exercise 1 in the box above. Keep your eyes on the central column of letters this time. What can you see on either side?

| | | |
|---|---|---|
| WG | H | PF |
| KD | T | OL |
| VS | K | DA |
| YO | E | NL |
| PZ | R | NJ |
| 5S | I | B9 |
| QP | K | BS |
| MG | T | MK |
| MO | R | EP |
| KR | X | KF |

## Exercise 3

Follow the instructions for Exercise 1 in the box above. This time keep your eyes on the central words.

| | | |
|---|---|---|
| only if | armbands | existed but |
| once a | bee | swam in |
| a three | legged | race he |
| got half | way | to the other |
| end of the | beer glass | but was |
| drunk | and was | never seen |
| again | the wasp | won by |
| default | the fly | lost the |
| bet | and nobody | lives for |
| ever | but | who knows. |

Did you find the words any easier to read than the random letters? The words didn't make much sense in themselves. Try the next exercise.

## Exercise 4

You are now beginning to read more than one word at a time.
Read the text as quickly as possible, keeping your eyes in the
middle of the pyramid.

A

beetle

loved a

certain hare

And wandered with him

everywhere:

They went to fairs

and feasts together,

Took walks in any kind of weather,

Talked of the future

and the past

On sunny days or overcast,

But since their friendship was so pleasant,

Lived for the most part in the present.

(From 'The Eagle and the Beetle', by Vikram Seth,
*Beastly Tales from Here and There*, Phoenix House)

### *READ WITH YOUR EYES INSTEAD OF YOUR EARS*

The next exercise illustrates the difference between reading with
your ears (ear-reading) and with your eyes (eye-reading). The more
you practise eye-reading, the better you will become at trusting
what you see without having to hear it.

**Exercise 5**

Try ear-reading and eye-reading:

1 *Cut a piece of thick card, about 2 cm square.*
2 *Place the card over each set of numbers and/or letters in the chart on page 119 and 'flash' the letter/number combination to yourself as quickly as you can.*
3 *Once you have covered each one up, write what you saw in the adjacent column.*
4 *Try to keep the pace at which you reveal the numbers and letters to yourself constant. If you started by flashing the first column to yourself at a set a second, aim to keep up the same speed when you reach the final column.*

Now check your answers against the printed characters:

▶ *Which column was easiest?*
▶ *Did you sometimes mistake an 'S' for a '5'?*
▶ *Were the double lines more challenging than the single lines?*
▶ *Were the letters that most resembled words immediately recognizable and easy to recall?*
▶ *Did you get some of the non-words that seemed like words wrong because you saw the first few letters and made the rest up? (e.g. Did you write John for Johm?)*

Develop your own eye exercises like the ones you have just tried and practise them as often as time allows. If you want to choose just one exercise to develop your visual reading for your 21-day programme (see Chapter 12), Exercise 5 should be the one.

| 143 | Emc2 | tdp 3Pq | inki blt9 |
| 146 | Lsp5 | 3owm olp | 286r wom8 |
| Heg | wini | tap cim | unIw te4q |
| 37R | rQwg | 536 592 | wim2 241y |
| 63I | 6The | per ith | tolp 154r |
| 53L | Hare | kin min | tosi 90Pp |
| Jo4 | M23p | map 43T | 76yz jipx |
| ThR | Luck | yat wea | Johm minz |
| 2h7 | 7play | mic 857 | jut7a ping |
| Jon | u89UN | fiy u8p | 683po joke |
| 8Em | Pking | 90L yum | jy97q jopt |
| Em2 | 43Jub | 738 kin | fyfe york |
| 492 | krimb | mop j46 | tunnl yonks |
| hEp | HatrP | moy 86w | 153tj mouse |
| Gep | 53Mot | 824 | jimbo |
| 9UB | buton | | |
| PL3 | 82L87 | | |
| pl3 | Ep26I | | |
| Tj4 | Grand | | |
| 96F | fa6me | | |
| Iy8 | Noma | | |
| iokO | Mcok1 | | |

## Reading more than one line at a time

This will take practice. When you read more than one line at a time you are doing something you may not have thought of doing before and you are doing something you may have thought impossible. If so, you may be working against your belief system. In situations like this, what you need is evidence. You will be able to provide yourself with your own evidence once you have taken a little time to practise the next exercise.

You began to experience what it was like to see more than one line at a time when you did Exercise 5 above. This can only be done effectively when you read with your eyes, not your ears. Remember the exercise on getting the message in Chapter 2 (see pp. 36–37). You found that if you saw the words in the wrong order you were still able to understand what the message was. This is the technique to use to practise this new skill.

To encourage your mind to see more than one line at a time, follow the steps outlined in the box below. When you begin you may find that your comprehension dips. This is to be expected. The more you practise, the more comfortable you will become with reading with your eyes instead of your ears.

### *EXERCISE TO LEARN HOW TO READ MORE THAN ONE LINE AT A TIME*

Set a timer for 3 minutes. When it goes off, re-set it for another 3 minutes. Continue until you have finished the exercise.

| First 3 minutes | Read one line at a time. | Read for good comprehension as fast as you can. Place your pacer under each line. |
|---|---|---|

| Second 3 minutes | Increase your range to two lines at a time. | Place your pacer under every second line. Move the pacer smoothly under the lines, seeing all the words. Your aim is to 'get the message' from the lines without reading all the words. |
| --- | --- | --- |
| Third 3 minutes | Increase your range to three lines. | Again, take in enough words to 'get the message' but avoid skimming for information. As you do this broaden your vision by looking at the margins on both sides of the text. Move the pacer at the same pace as you have been for one and two lines. |
| Fourth 3 minutes | Increase your range to four lines. | Your aim is still to 'get the message' as fast as you can without hearing the words in your mind. Make sure you are seeing all the words and recognizing them as you move down the page. Remember to relax and enjoy the experience of learning something new. |
| Fifth 3 minutes | Increase your reading range to five lines at a time. | You may be looking at a whole paragraph at a time now. Let your eyes see everything and find out if you can pick out the message. |
| Finally | Go back to reading one line at a time. | Use your pacer and read as fast as you can for good comprehension. What difference do you notice in your reading now? |

## EXERCISE TO INCREASE PERIPHERAL VISION AND AWARENESS

Take a short walk. As you walk, look straight ahead.
Try to see as much as you can in your whole visual range.
What is in the extremes of your visual field, left and right,
top and bottom? Articulate what you see as you see it. After
you have done this for a while, sit down and, using a pacer,
read as fast as you can for good comprehension. Notice the
difference in the speed and ease of your reading. This is an
excellent exercise to do while you are walking through town
or in a park.

## Making your peripheral vision work for you

When you read, apply what you learned in your walk
through the park. Remember how much you could see and
make good use of your visual energy. Reading one word
at a time places your focus on the first word of every line,
which means that much of what you see is the empty space
in the margins. So, instead of aiming your eye at the start
of the line, aim it about two words into the line and let your
peripheral perception do the work.

## How to prevent and cure eyestrain

## Experiment

Here is an experiment to show you how your eyesight
deteriorates through strain.

Stare at a page. Do not blink or move your eyes. How long is it before your vision begins to blur or your eyes begin to water? It doesn't take much to strain your eyes.

Resting your eyes, blinking and taking care of yourself will prevent eyestrain. Your eyes need rest. The more relaxed they are, the longer you will be able to read.

These few simple procedures will help you prevent and cure eyestrain:

▶ *Before you feel tired, rest your eyes by* **closing** *them for a few moments every 10 or 15 minutes.*
▶ *As often as you remember to, try* **palming.** *Palming is an excellent eye-relaxing exercise. Rub your hands together until they are warm, then close your eyes and cover them with your hands so that no light gets in. Do not press against your eyeballs: that could damage them. Cover your eyes like this for 10–15 minutes.*
▶ *Spend some time in the* **sun.** *The natural rays of the sun can revitalize your eyes and are an excellent source of Vitamin D, needed by your eyes to remain healthy. All you have to do is close your eyes and turn them towards the sun. Do not open your eyes and look directly at the sun. In hot, tropical parts of the world, do this for only a few minutes. In northern climates you can face the sun for a little longer. Sunning your eyes will ease bloodshot eyes and decrease irritability and itchiness. If there is no sun, use an incandescent source of light (one that produces some warmth) instead.*
▶ **Blink.** *The scratchy feeling in your eyes may be because they are dry. Many people with eye problems compound them by not blinking and watering their eyes. While you are reading (especially from a PC monitor) be aware of your eyes and blink often. If it helps, put a sign above your PC reminding yourself to blink.*
▶ **Swinging** *is an exercise that not only relaxes your eyes but relaxes your whole body as well. Stand at a window or outside (anywhere you can get a long-distance view) and swing your body and head from side to side, moving your eyes across the whole horizon. Focus in turn on everything that comes into*

*your visual field, no matter how close or far away it is. Relax, think of something happy and comfortable and enjoy the break from whatever you were doing.*

▶ **Change your focus.** *Stand where you have a long-distance view. Hold your thumb about 15 cm from your eyes. First focus on your thumb and then change your focus to look at the furthest point from you. Do this slowly and gently. If you have been looking at a PC or reading for a long time, your eyes will be tired and changing your focus too quickly could give you a headache. Relax and take your time.*

▶ *If your eyes feel particularly tired there are various* **eyewashes** *available that you can get from any pharmacy. Follow the instructions carefully when you use them. Check with your optician or your doctor if the problem persists.*

▶ *If you wear* **contact lenses** *it is particularly important to take good care of your eyes while you are reading. If you have a lot of reading to do it may be advisable to wear spectacles instead. Always have a pair of glasses with you so that you can take out your lenses if your eyes get uncomfortable.*

▶ *While reading, your eyes are limited to how much they move around the text or screen. An excellent way to relieve the tension that this causes is by practising* **eye-robics.** *First look straight ahead, then look up as far as you can, down as far as you can, then to the left and then to the right. Next look to the top left, top right, bottom right and bottom left. Hold each gaze for only a second or so. When you have done that, squeeze your eyes shut and, if you want to, repeat the exercise. After you have completed the exercise, palm for a few minutes.*

▶ **Acupressure** *is very relaxing and very good for your eyes (see p. 125).*

You may find when you try acupressure that the area around your eyes feels sensitive and sometimes a little painful. This is due to tension there. You have the same sensitivity when you have a stiff neck and someone gives you a massage – at some points it is more pain than pleasure!

Never rub your eyes directly on the eyeball. There is nothing to protect the eye from damage if you do that.

## Acupressure

1 Close your eyes and rest your elbows comfortably on a table.

2 Use your thumbs to massage the inside corners of your eyebrows (8 seconds).

3 Use your thumb and index finger to massage the bridge of your nose (8 seconds).

4 Massage the area of your cheekbone directly under the centre of your eye (8 seconds).

5 Using your three middle fingers, press firmly but gently all around the bony ridge around your eye socket, moving in a clockwise direction (8 times around your eyes).

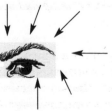

6 Keeping your eyes closed, palm for a few minutes, stretch and carry on with what you were doing.

# Reading from a PC monitor

## *AVOID STRAINING YOUR EYES*

There is much you can do to make reading from a monitor less stressful on your eyes. Here are a few tips:

- ▶ **Font type and size** – *If someone has sent you a document and the font is difficult to read due to either its size or type, change it.*
- ▶ **Screen contrast** – *Make sure the background is a contrast to the text on the screen. For some people a white screen may be too strong and for others a blue one may be too dark. Experiment with different screen colours. A pale blue or grey background is worth a try.*
- ▶ **Light** – *There is a misconception that natural light is good when working at a monitor. Natural light is uneven and moves as the sun shifts in the sky and shadows change. This affects your screen and can cause eyestrain. Also, the glare of the sun on your screen may make reading very difficult. If you don't move your screen when working in natural light you may begin to suffer from back problems due to shifting about and sitting in awkward positions to enable you to view the screen.*
- ▶ **Screen interference** – *Have as little distraction on your screen as possible. It may be tempting to have all the icons on display. The more you have on your screen, the smaller the reading and writing space will be. Only have what is necessary for the work you are doing.*
- ▶ **Screen savers** – *There are screen savers on the market now that remain active all the time. One that took my attention was a sheep that ran around the screen while I worked. Not only did it help to relax my eyes and prevent me from staring at the screen, but a sheep chasing frogs across the screen was good for my sense of humour. Anything good for your sense of humour is good for your stress levels, which in turn is good for concentration.*

- ▶ **Screen position** – *Have the screen a comfortable distance away from you. It should be at least an arm's length away. Avoid having the screen directly in front of a window – the contrast in light may be uncomfortable and activity outside can be distracting.*
- ▶ **Comfort** – *Working at a PC means that the only parts of your body that get any exercise are your fingers. Stop, stretch your body and do the eye-robics every 20 to 30 minutes.*

### SPEED READING FROM A MONITOR

- ▶ **Use the arrow as a pacer** – *Instead of moving it along each line, which can make it difficult to follow, pull the arrow down the middle of the page or in an 'S' shape.*
- ▶ **Change the margins** – *If you find it easier to read whole lines at a time when they are narrower than a full page, change the margins of the text to make the written text narrower and easier to read.*
- ▶ **Make everything single spaced** – *Information can be read faster single spaced than when the text is double or triple spaced.*
- ▶ *If you use your 'page down' key to get from one page to the next you will waste time by having to find where you were before the page jumped.* **Scrolling down** *not only avoids the jumps but also provides you with a pacer in the shape of the bottom of the screen.*

## Eye nutrition

Like your memory and concentration, your eyes are greatly affected by what you eat. One rule applies: what is good for your heart is also good for your eyes. The following supplements have been shown to have a beneficial effect on eyesight.

| Supplement | What it does | Consequence of a shortage | Sources |
|---|---|---|---|
| Vitamin A, beta carotene | The eyes need these for night vision. They also help your eyes to adjust when exposed to flickering fluorescent lights, heat, glare, computer monitors and television sets. Smoking and alcohol deplete Vitamin A. | Reduced night vision. | Oranges, green vegetables. |
| Vitamin B complex | Thiamin (Vitamin B1) keeps the eye muscles working. Riboflavin (B2) keeps eyes at correct light sensitivity level. Vitamin B6 is involved in emotional balance. Vitamin B12 may protect against some serious eye conditions. | If you have a shortage of Vitamin B2 you may find that your eyes burn, you have a sensitivity to bright lights and you feel unusually tired. A shortage of it is found in some cataract patients. A lack of Vitamin B12 shows up in cataract and glaucoma sufferers. | Dark green vegetables, brewer's yeast, eggs, meat, nuts and seeds. |

| Supplement | What it does | Consequence of a shortage | Sources |
|---|---|---|---|
| Vitamin C, containing ascorbic acid and bioflavinoids | Good for circulation in the eyes. Smoking depletes Vitamin C. | Poor circulation. | Citrus fruit, tomatoes, melons. |
| Vitamin D and calcium | Some nutritionists believe that the consumption of excess sugar is a major cause of near-sightedness. A lower sugar intake and an increase in calcium intake may help those with this problem. | Possibly near-sightedness, detached retina and glaucoma. | Sunlight, milk. |
| Vitamin E | Helps the blood stream carry oxygen and nutrition to the rest of the body. It also seems to be important for maintaining the elasticity of the eye muscles. | Near-sightedness. | Avocado pear, green/black olives, sunflower seeds, coconuts, cold pressed virgin olive oil. |

# TEN THINGS TO REMEMBER

1   *If you have a lot of web-based material to read, apologize to the trees and print it out. It will save your eyes (and you a lot of time).*

2   *Make sure the lighting is good.*

3   *Remind yourself to blink, especially if you're reading off a PC screen.*

4   *To ease eyestrain close your eyes and cover them with the palms of your hands.*

5   *Using a pacer will prevent your eyes bouncing around the page too much.*

6   *During a reading session take time to lift your gaze and look at the horizon or some distant point.*

7   *If you're reading off the PC screen, change the settings to increase the font size.*

8   *Take care of your eyes. Any discomfort is a warning. Drink plenty of water. Go for a walk. Relax a little.*

9   *If you've been working at a PC all day do yourself a favour and don't watch too much TV at night.*

10  *Get plenty of quality sleep.*

# 8

# Distractions and solutions

In this chapter you will learn:
- *how to combat external, internal and physical distractions*

## Insight
All distractions, no matter what their source, only become distractions when you let them. What goes on around you is just a series of events. How you let them impact your attention is up to you and where you place your priorities.

In an ideal world we would read only what interested us, only in the right environment, only when we had as much time as we needed, and only when we wanted to. Life is not like that. We must often read material we are not particularly interested in, at a time and place not suited to our reading style and, all too often, with a deadline.

Distractions are not just what happens around you. Your internal state can be as distracting as a constantly ringing telephone. Distractions hamper effective reading and accurate recall. The more you can reduce them, the more chance you will have of successfully reading what you need to in the time you have available.

In this chapter we shall explore a range of distractions and ways of working around them.

## Lack of concentration

If your attention drifts easily, seemingly inconsequential things distract you, and you find it hard to concentrate, there may be an easy solution.

We discussed concentration in Chapter 4. If you think it may be helpful to go back to refresh your memory, try one of the concentration exercises in that chapter (see pp. 65–70). The following tips will also help you increase your concentration and your ability to focus on one task:

▶ *To ensure peak concentration,* **take breaks often** *– approximately 5 minutes every 30 minutes if you are reading only. If you are reading a number of different texts and taking notes you could stretch your reading time to between 45 minutes and 1 hour before you take a 5- or 10-minute break. Pay attention to your body as you read. When you start yawning, making mistakes or re-reading passages, or if you develop a headache, it is time for a break. If you work through the symptoms of tiredness your concentration, and your ability to remember and understand what you are reading will diminish rapidly. Taking a break does not mean lying down and going to sleep for 20 minutes (although that does help) – you can go for a walk, drink some water, simply do something different.*

▶ *Know your* **reasons for reading***. The clearer your purpose, the easier it will be to concentrate even if you do not really want to. If you have no reason, you will probably give up fairly quickly.*

▶ **Read actively** *using a pacer, especially if you are feeling tired or if the material is challenging. The more senses you use, the more alert you are likely to remain. Imagine having a meal when all you can do is look at it. You can't smell it, taste it, feel the texture of the food or hear the sounds of cutting, slicing and chewing. All you can do is see it and eat it. How much do you think you would enjoy that meal?*

*Eighty per cent of the enjoyment of a meal is in the sensory appreciation of it: the taste, smell, texture and presentation of the food. The same applies to reading. Unfortunately we are taught at a very early age to appreciate reading only through one sense. When you start building mind-maps, taking notes, thinking about what you read, discussing and actively reading, you will find that reading becomes more like the meal you can see, taste, smell, hear and feel. You almost always remember a good meal when the company is good and the surroundings pleasant. Treat reading like a good meal – you'll be surprised at what happens.*

▶ *Set a definite* **time limit**. *Break your reading into 30-minute chunks. The chunks should be small enough to feel easily manageable and big enough to feel that you are achieving your goal. Be realistic. If as you read you find that the size of chunks is too big or too small, stop and reassess. Be flexible.*

## COPING WITH EXTERNAL NOISE

If you are not one of those people who concentrates either because of, or in spite of, background noise, you need to do everything you can to minimize the noise around you. Unfortunately, there is always likely to be some external noise you don't have much control over. If you work in an open-plan office you may find the noise distracting.

There are several things you can do to minimize distraction from this kind of noise:

▶ **Earplugs** – *If you get the right type they can be very comfortable and effective. Most good chemists will supply them. Try out a few makes, then keep several sets of them in your desk.*

▶ *Wear earphones and play appropriate* **music** *through them – music without words and not too loud. Baroque music is best for maximum concentration. Make sure what you listen to is not too melancholy and only play music you enjoy. Mozart, Vivaldi and some of Beethoven's works are especially good for concentration. You can experiment with music. Put one composer on for 20 minutes, change to another and then* *compare how you feel or how well you concentrated. (See p. 64 for some specific suggestions.)*

▶ *If your desk is in a truly* **open-plan space** *with no dividers between the desks, creating a visual barrier between you and the rest of the space will help cut distraction. You do not have to build a wall around you – this is not always desirable or possible. All you need to do is place something on your desk that reaches eye level. This will provide a psychological barrier between you and the distracting environment and make it easier to cope with.*

▶ *If at all possible, leave the noisy environment and find a quiet space to read in.*

## Insight

A delegate in one of my workshops used to go into the cleaner's cupboard when he had a document to read that needed all his attention. He would disappear into the cupboard and emerge when he was done. It need not be a cupboard... but find yourself a private space.

### COPING WITH INTERNAL NOISE

Internal noise is caused by your mind wandering, perhaps because you have not decided to spend the time on a particular task. The advice on concentration in Chapter 4 will help you here. What will help most, however, is the decision to take the time to read.

If you don't make a firm decision to sit down and read, the type of internal talk that goes through your head might sound like this: 'I don't have the time for this ... X really needs to be done now ... Y will have to move to this afternoon ... I should be doing Z ...' There will be so much noise in your head that you will be unlikely to remember one word you have read and will be wasting time.

▶ *Make a decision to allocate a certain amount of time to read a set amount of material. If you can plan it into your day, do so. Some reading cannot be planned for. In this instance, instead of diving into the text without thinking, take time to go through the preparation and preview stages quickly. Then if you think that the document really does need to be read, decide when you are going to do it and put the time aside.*

▶ *After the decision is made, most internal talk will disappear and you will be able to focus.*

## Physical distractions

### *TIREDNESS*

When you are tired it will be almost impossible to concentrate. If you can, take a break and have a short nap or go for a walk in the park. If you are unable to do that, there are several other strategies open to you:

▶ *Cut the time you spend reading down to 10–15-minute chunks.*
▶ *Use multi-sensory reading.*
▶ *Drink plenty of water.*
▶ *Do aerobic exercises during your breaks – jump up and down a bit to get the oxygen flowing.*
▶ *Breathe deeply and stretch every few minutes.*
▶ *If you have music playing make it upbeat and energetic.*
▶ *Make sure you have a very good reason if you read through your tiredness.*
▶ *Do not go on longer than you have to – stop when you are finished and have a good rest.*
▶ *Avoid working through the night.*
▶ *Avoid excess sugar or starch.*
▶ *Avoid caffeine. For maximum performance you want to be alert, not jittery.*
▶ *As we have seen in Chapter 4, reading at the right time of day can go a long way to preventing tiredness. You may notice that you can concentrate better at certain times of day than others. Your results will be better if you read at those times.*

### SORE EYES

Any kind of physical discomfort is a distraction. Your eyes are your primary tool for reading; take care of them. Refresh your memory about eye care by reading the summary at the end of Chapter 7.

### STRESS AND READING

If you are stressed it is better to stop for a short time, even if you think you don't have the time. Stop, breathe, relax, evaluate the job, have a caffeine-free drink or some water and carry on. Being stressed does not make most people read any faster or more effectively.

### HUNGER AND THIRST

Hunger is a serious distraction. Conversely, if you eat too much your concentration will be impaired. If you have a large amount of reading to do, avoid eating too much at once and avoid excess sugar and starch.

Another cause of poor concentration is dehydration. Your body is 90 per cent water, and by the time you feel thirsty you are already dehydrated. Drink plenty of water even if you don't feel you need any. Avoid tea and coffee – the caffeine in them will dehydrate you still more.

---

## Environmental issues

### COMFORT

Ensure you have fresh air and adequate light. Make yourself as comfortable as possible without becoming sleepy.

### LIGHT

Daylight is best (unless you are using a PC). If there is none, then there should not be much contrast between the levels of light under which you are working and the rest of the room. This helps prevent eyestrain. A general rule is that the main source of light should come over the shoulder opposite to your writing hand.

### DESK AND CHAIR

Make sure your desk and chair are the right height. When you sit on the chair you should be able to sit back, supporting your back with your feet flat on the floor. If you cannot reach the floor place a block at your feet. Your desk should be large enough to take everything you need for the work you are undertaking.

---

## Work distractions

Here is some general advice about coping with distractions at work:

▶ **Plan your day** – *Distractions come easily when you don't know what you want to achieve. At the start of your day write down everything you want to achieve, including the reading you want to do. Set aside time for it. It might also be useful to put time aside in your plan for leisure reading. Once you plan it and you can see that reading a novel for a while isn't going to mean that you will not achieve everything else in your day, you will find that you enjoy the time, still get everything done and improve your speed reading by reading more.*

▶ **Set ground-rules** – *Once you start something, don't let anything distract you from completing it unless there is a very good reason. Have you ever started mowing the lawn or doing the dishes, only to get distracted onto something else and then find you don't really want to go back to what you started? Once you start something, finish it. This will not only improve the quality of your work, it will increase the quantity you can achieve. You will also feel more relaxed and at ease because the job has been done.*

## PEOPLE DEMANDING YOUR ATTENTION

Few people have the luxury of being able to work without interruption. There will almost always be someone, somewhere demanding your attention at some point, whether by phone, in person or by e-mail.

If you can, set aside the time you need to read. Put up a 'Do not disturb' notice. If you are unable to do that – and most of us are – deal with interruptions like phone calls and people wanting to see you by consciously breaking off from your reading task and paying attention to the interruption.

If the phone rings or someone comes up to you while you are reading:

> ▶ *If possible, finish the sentence or paragraph you are on.*
> ▶ *Place a mark on the place where you stopped.*
> ▶ *Briefly revise in your mind or on paper your understanding of the last sentence you read.*
> ▶ *Then give attention to the next task.*

Once the interruption is over, you can return to your reading:

> ▶ *Sit for a moment and recall your understanding of the last sentence you read.*
> ▶ *Re-affirm your intention and purpose for reading.*
> ▶ *Set the time again for a manageable chunk.*
> ▶ *Continue to read.*

Habit dictates that when we are interrupted we are very likely to hop from one task to another. Instead of doing this, take a brief pause between tasks. Ensure that you don't waste time trying to find where you left off before the distraction; doing this will prevent you from having to sort out your ideas and avoid confusion in your mind when you get back to the task.

## Clearing your desk of distractions

It is important to avoid distracting yourself with other tasks:

▶ **Mail** – *If you get a lot of mail at the beginning of the day have a routine of no more than 20 minutes each day to open all your mail and file it, deal with it or bin it. Don't let anything get in the way of doing that. It might not seem an important job at the time but when a week's mail piles up on your desk, undealt with, it can be very distracting. It may make you waste more time than you spend in dealing with it in a daily session.*

▶ **E-mail** – *Try to deal with all your e-mail at one point in the day.*

▶ **Desk space** – *Every piece of paper on your desk may distract you several times every day. To minimize this type of distraction make sure that the only things on your desk are those that have something to do with the project in hand. If you have your In and Out trays on your desk, find another place for them for a week. At the end of the week, assess how differently you spent your time. As long as the tray is on your desk, you only have to look up and you will see everything else you have to do that day instead of being able to focus on one job at a time.*

▶ **Clutter** – *If your desk tends to be covered with paper, clear it of everything other than the job at hand for just one day. Note the difference. At the end of each day, make sure you leave your desk totally clear. In the morning you will feel far more relaxed and able to choose what you want to deal with instead of having to deal with whatever happens to be on the top of the pile.*

▶ **Other people's reading** – *Do not let anyone put anything on your desk that you haven't seen and agreed to have there, especially if you have to read it. When someone gives you something to read ask them to explain clearly why they think you should read it, then decide if you want to accept it as an activity in your schedule. If they cannot give you a satisfactory reason, think carefully before you accept it; once you do, you will have to commit yourself to the time required to doing it.*

# TEN THINGS TO REMEMBER

1 Determine exactly where the distraction is coming from (internal or external) and deal with it.

2 Take plenty of breaks.

3 Use earplugs in a noisy environment.

4 If you work in an open-plan office, create a barrier between you and people around you with files and plants.

5 Beat internal noise (you talking to yourself), by focusing on your purpose and setting a time limit.

6 Be well rested and suitably fed. Tiredness and hunger are great distracters.

7 Remember to breathe deep.

8 Set ground rules: make the task of reading a priority and don't let anything else distract you.

9 If the phone rings while you're reading, take a moment to mark where you stopped reading before you answer it. Better yet, don't answer it – let them leave a message.

10 Don't let other people dictate where your concentration should be.

# 9

# Real-world reading

In this chapter you will learn:
- *how to read under pressure*
- *how to make the most of your available time*
- *how to find information fast*
- *how to reduce unnecessary reading*
- *how to evaluate your progress*

How often have you read a book on speed reading and thought that the ideas outlined would be all very well if you had the luxury of working in your own environment? Reading in the real world means that you don't always have peace and solitude to concentrate on what you are doing. You are almost certain to be interrupted and you will probably have a deadline that is too close for comfort. This chapter presents some ideas on how to read under pressure.

## Information bottleneck

Sometimes you have more to read than you have time for and you never seem to get to the end. Two possible explanations are:

▶ *You feel you need to know everything.*
▶ *Procrastination.*

### NEED TO KNOW

If you find that you have more reading to do than you can cope with, ask yourself a question: 'Do I really need all of this information or am I reading it because I'm worried that if I don't know it all I'll not be able to do my job well or help others do theirs?' Be sure to answer this honestly.

> ## Insight
> Fear is the great driver in this behaviour: fear of appearing ignorant, foolish or out of the loop. Everyone feels this at some point. Admitting you don't know (but that you can find out) does your credibility far more good than holding back because you don't want to seem uninformed.

A number of other attitudes are connected with the urge to know everything.

### Apparent urgency
You may be in the habit of dealing with something as soon as you receive it, no matter what else has to be done or how important the latest task really is. If someone gives you a document to read and says, 'This is urgent, you must read it now', don't take their word for it. According to them it may be urgent, but it might be the second or third most urgent thing in your day. Take the time to prioritize.

### Nobody does it better
This is an excellent attitude if you want to make sure you have plenty of work to do every weekend and holiday. Most people are capable of doing their jobs well. Think positively, have faith in others, prioritize and delegate.

### Generosity
When it comes to your own time, you cannot always afford to be generous. Often the people who give you something extra to deal with are doing so to avoid doing it themselves.

### PROCRASTINATION

Two causes of procrastination are fear and a lack of interest. If you have a task to do and it seems big or challenging, you may do other seemingly important things instead of facing the situation and dealing with it.

The cure for this is straightforward. Determine exactly what the job entails instead of letting your imagination drive you further away from it. Once you know what is involved, break the job into small chunks and deal with it a piece at a time.

## Insight

Instead of allowing your in-tray to overflow, do the five steps on every document as soon as it arrives. Even if you don't read it completely, you will have an accurate evaluation of what it's about which will prevent your imagination from turning it into more than it is.

If the cause of the procrastination is lack of interest, find something in it that will motivate you. If you can find nothing and your desk is always full of paperwork that needs to be dealt with but you can't be bothered to do it, then you may want to consider a different job.

Being an information bottleneck does not do anyone any good. Information should flow freely throughout an organization. Once you enlist the help of others and share information you will be surprised at how much you can achieve to get things moving.

## Prioritizing and planning

More often than not, a lack of prioritization is the cause of a desk full of reading that you cannot get through. When the pile gets too high, you begin to feel that you can't do anything and begin to suffer from 'paper fatigue' – you feel exhausted every time you go near your desk. The better you prioritize your reading, the faster you will get through it.

When you prioritize, the risk of falling into the trap of becoming an information bottleneck will decrease. Although it might take you a little time if you are starting from scratch, once you get used to prioritizing you will do it naturally on a daily basis.

Whether you are starting with a pile of collected paperwork or dealing with your daily mail, following these simple steps will help you prioritize effectively:

▶ *Gather all your reading or paperwork together.*
▶ *Sort it into three piles: urgent, important, other.*
▶ *Go through each pile and determine what the pay-off for dealing with each bit of paper will be (see next step).*
▶ *Ask this question to help you determine the nature of the pay-off. Are you reading the document for profit, to meet a deadline or to achieve a goal? If you have a pile full of documents that seem urgent but don't have much of a pay-off, consider whether each really is urgent or whether it is in the pile because someone said it should be there.*
▶ *Write an action list of everything you need to read in order of priority. Note down how long each one is likely to take you, why you think you need to read it and what you are going to get from or achieve by reading it.*
▶ *Plan your reading into your day according to when you need the information. Reading something you are going to use in a few weeks' time may mean that when you are closer to requiring the information you will have to revise it anyway. You might as well wait until later (sometimes procrastinating is the right thing to do).*

### MAKING THE MOST OF THE TIME YOU HAVE AVAILABLE

The most important thing about reading for work or study (this advice does not apply to leisure reading unless you want it to) is planning. These are simple guidelines on how to make the most of your time:

▶ *Read when you are feeling alert and refreshed. If you have to read and you are tired, drink plenty of water and take regular breaks.*
▶ *Plan what you have to read and set aside a little more time than you think you will need to do it.*

- ▶ *When someone puts something on your desk expecting you to read it, find out whether it is really necessary and whether someone can summarize it for you so that you do not have to read the whole document yourself.*
- ▶ *Make the bin the first option when you are sorting mail (including e-mail).*
- ▶ *When you are going through your mail decide what you have to read and put non-urgent documents aside. If you have time at the end of the day to read them, then do so.*

## Coping with meetings

'I only have five minutes and I have to sound as if I know what I'm talking about.' Have you ever said this? Many of us find ourselves in the situation where someone gives us a document and tells us that we are expected at a meeting very soon to discuss it with others who have had a day or so to read it.

You could bluff your way through if others know less than you do, but eventually you would probably be caught out. It's better to find a reading strategy that gives you a chance of absorbing vital information than to struggle to look as if you know what you are talking about.

Do you find that in these circumstances your mind goes blank and for some reason words and letters don't make sense any more? This has more to do with stress and a lack of strategy than it does with time. When this happens:

- ▶ *Ask the person handing you the document what it has to do with you – get background information.*
- ▶ *Ask them why you only have 5 minutes – this gives you an idea of the purpose and focus.*
- ▶ *Ask them to summarize briefly the text for you – this gives you the content.*

Once you have done that, complete Steps 1 to 4 of the five-step system (prepare, preview, passive and active reading):

▶ *Determine your purpose – why do you have to read this? What are you going to do with the information?*
▶ *Flip through the text, reading any summaries or conclusions.*
▶ *Read through it passively, this time looking for key words and significant figures or words in bold or italics.*
▶ *Read the first and last paragraphs of each section actively.*

If there is time, use it to fill in the gaps by reading as much as you can, beginning with the first sentence of each paragraph and any bullet points.

## Very important

As you go through Steps 1 to 4, take notes – preferably on the document itself. The thoughts you have as you read will probably be what you would want to contribute to the meeting. If you don't write them down you may forget and lose valuable insights.

### GOING INTO THE MEETING

### Insight

My primary advice is to avoid them. Most are an absolute waste of time where real issues are hardly ever fully discussed or resolved. But if you insist on attending meetings...

Before you go into the meeting, stop at the door, stand up straight, breathe in deeply, smile and relax. Once you are inside:

▶ *Don't profess to be an expert on the subject unless you are!*

▶ *Listen first to what others have to say.*
▶ *Ask questions before you make statements.*

Once you take control you will relax and be able to concentrate on the meeting.

---

## Finding information fast

There are many occasions when you have to find information fast. To do this you can use Steps 1, 2 and 3 of the five-step system (prepare, preview and passive reading). These can be broken down into the following stages:

1 *Be very clear about what you are looking for.*
2 *Write your purpose down.*
3 *Begin Step 2 (preview) by highlighting any chapters or sections that look as if they may contain the answers to your questions. Use Post-it notes to mark the relevant pages, writing a comment on them to show what you expect to find there.*
4 *Once Step 2 is completed, begin Step 3 (passive reading) by re-stating and re-clarifying your purpose. What exactly are you looking for and what are the key words that would alert you to the answer?*
5 *Passively read (skim or scan) the pieces of text you identified during the preview stage.*
6 *Stop as soon as you find your answer – unless you decide to continue.*

### RETRIEVING INFORMATION

When you read a document for the first time, read it with the intention of going back to it to find information at a later date. Mark relevant pages or take referencing notes. Writing a brief summary of each section in the margin is an excellent way to help you access information later. It is also a very good technique for remembering what you have read.

### READING UNDER PRESSURE

A deadline can be one of the biggest distractions. Becoming wound up and stressed only defeats the object. When you have such a situation:

1 *Make a realistic assessment of the time available.*
2 *Decide what you have to know.*
3 *Decide what the best and fastest source of information is.*
4 *If it is something you have to read, complete Steps 1 to 3 of the five-step system (prepare, preview and passive reading) and be very disciplined about cutting out what is not essential.*
5 *Speak to someone who already knows something about the subject and gather as much information as possible from them.*
6 *Find out exactly why you have such a tight deadline and see whether it can be changed.*
7 *After your questions have been answered, divide your reading into the amount of time you have. Focus, relax, breathe deeply and make sure you have a good supply of water.*
8 *Take plenty of breaks. It is more important to sit back and take stock when you are under pressure than when you have all the time in the world. If you are under pressure and not taking care of yourself, stress will counteract all the work you are doing.*

## New jobs, projects and clients

In a new situation – whether you are dealing with a fresh job, project or client – you need to find out just what you need to know.

### NEW SUBJECT OR PROJECT – FAMILIAR CLIENT

If you are working on a job where the client (who may be your employer or an external client) has asked you to do work that is outside your area of expertise, you will still be expected to provide a professional service. You have a learning curve to go through before you even begin. To make the task easier, here are some ideas:

▶ *Start with Step 1 of the five-step system – **prepare**. Determine exactly what the job is. Write down everything you already know, everything you are expected to know, what questions you have, where you are likely to find the answers and what gaps you are aware of in your knowledge.*

▶ *Then find out the **level of expertise** required. You may have to hire the services of an expert to complete the job satisfactorily. If you determine that the level of expertise is within your grasp, **commit** yourself to doing the job well.*

▶ *When you have done that, speak to your employer, the client or an expert in the field and find out what the **best source of information** is.*

▶ *Gather together the material that may contain the information you need and **follow the five-step system** to get as much information as possible out of it. Devote a little time to doing nothing but learning.*

▶ ***Speak** to people about the job. This is a good way to make sure you stay on track and stay motivated.*

▶ *Subscribe to a **specialist magazine** and get as many different views as possible on the subject.*

▶ *Avoid breaking the job down into 'learning' and 'doing' phases (except for the period of time right at the beginning). Commit yourself to **learning** all the way through instead.*

▶ *Keep **reference cards** for information gained. Divide the cards into 'need to know', 'like to know' and 'interesting but not vital to know'.*

▶ *Keep a **record** of your progress and a notebook for questions you want to find answers to.*

▶ *Enjoy the exercise and treat it as an **exploration**. The less pressure you attach to the job, the easier it will be for you to learn and perform professionally.*

## FAMILIAR PROJECT OR SUBJECT – NEW CLIENT

This situation works the other way round when the task is familiar and the client is not. Instead of your attention being focused on the job, your attention should be focused on the client. You know what the job you are being asked to do entails. You should be asking yourself how what you know fits into what your client wants. The research you carry out should be on who your client is and how they work:

- ▶ *What market are they in?*
- ▶ *Have they commissioned work like this before?*
- ▶ *Do they know what to expect or is the field totally new to them?*
- ▶ *Are they doing the work because they want to (business development) or because they have to (business survival)? This will determine their attitude towards what you do and the level of detail you have to go into. A business working on survival will probably ask for the minimum because that may be all they have the time or budget for. A strong, growing business may have more time and money to spend.*
- ▶ *What do they already know about what you do?*
- ▶ *How involved will they be?*
- ▶ *Will they want to know how you do it or will the finished product be all they want to see?*

Gather all this information together. Go to the client, collect their literature and read their web site. Speak to the receptionists and assistants; they almost always know what is going on because they deal with more than one job or department at a time.

### NEW JOB, NEW CLIENT

This is challenging. Not only do you not know what you are doing but also you don't know who you are doing it for. If you have just started a new job you may be feeling like this.

To make the transition smooth and successful:

- ▶ *Follow the steps outlined in both of the above sections.*
- ▶ *Join professional societies who can provide you with information and training if you need it.*

▶ *Read Chapter 10, Working and studying for a living. Studying to get to grips with a new job can be more challenging than studying to pass an exam; in this case the 'exam' is continuous and the stakes are higher. The more you know, the better you will be able to perform. Read, ask questions and be responsible for your own professional development.*

## Insight

Don't assume that just because someone has been working with a company for a few years that they know what they're talking about. Be politely suspicious of everyone and get corroboration on everything.

## A plan for reducing your reading

Simply reducing the amount you read will save you an enormous amount of time.

If you don't need any particular types of report or memo, contact the sender and ask them not to send these to you any more. Internal mail that has nothing to do with you can be just as time consuming as junk mail.

## Reduce your reading

1 Collect up all the reports and memos you have on your desk or that require your attention.
2 Count the number of pages and determine how long it would take you to read them all (this will give you the motivation to find a better way of dealing with them).
3 Look at the reports and memos and find out if there is a pattern to them. Are they coming from the same person or office? Are they vital to your job? Do you have any interest in the subject matter? Do they arrive

*(Contd)*

regularly without your asking for them? Have you requested them? If you have, for what purpose?

**4** Carry out the second step (preview) on the reports by studying their structure. Are they written in such a way that you can gather the information you need without having to read the whole document? If you were to read only the summaries and conclusions, how long would it take you and would it be sufficient? If you don't read a whole report, does the person who wrote it know this? By telling them you may save them some time.

**5** Study the pile and determine how many decisions you have to make in relation to them. If you find that most of the reports and memos are for your information only and you don't have to do anything with them afterwards, the apparent urgency and importance of most of them will immediately diminish.

**6** Ask yourself whether you would be able to get the information that is in the report or memo just as effectively by speaking to someone for a few minutes.

**7** Another question to ask is whether the information in the report will be valid by the time you need it. Also ask if the information it contains is old news to you.

**8** If you are not sure whether you need to read a report or memo, put it aside on a trial basis. If after a while someone comes in asking you to act on it, you will know that you have to pay attention to it in the near future.

In future, as soon as a report or memo comes to your attention, go through it quickly asking yourself whether you need it. Add it to your reduction pile in the bin if you don't.

## Insight

A very successful colleague has a definite attitude towards mail, reports and memos: everything goes straight into the bin. His philosophy is that if it is important someone will come and see him or phone him. It is a high-risk strategy, but it has worked for him!

# Evaluating your progress

When you learn something new it is easy to get into a routine of simply doing it and forgetting to evaluate your progress to make sure that you are going in the right direction. It is fairly common for old habits and new (bad) habits to creep into your reading strategies even though you are practising a new and better way of reading. To make sure that you are continually improving, occasionally go back to the beginning to ensure that the foundation of your strategy is correct.

This is the real world, though. We don't always have the time or the inclination to go back and re-learn what we spent time learning in the first place. To reinforce the foundations easily:

▶ *Spend 5 minutes every few weeks doing a short speed reading test. Select a number of books or texts, all on different subjects and of varying difficulty, and follow the steps to measure your reading rate, outlined in Chapter 2 (p. 25).*
▶ *Keep a log of how well you are doing. If your reading speed or your comprehension is going down, spend some time that day or during the same week being aware of the strategies you are using and how you can improve them.*
▶ *If your reading speed and comprehension are going down, the most likely reason is that you are falling into the habit of not being aware while you are reading. Remember the exercises to increase and improve concentration (pp. 65–70). Do them as often as you can and select one that you are able to do daily.*
▶ *At the start of your day, when you plan your activities, make one of the activities effective and efficient reading. If you make yourself aware of your reading at the beginning of the day, you will notice that you are more aware of it throughout the day.*

# TEN THINGS TO REMEMBER

**1** *Don't procrastinate. Just because a document looks daunting doesn't mean it is.*

**2** *Don't feel under pressure to know everything.*

**3** *Make decisions about information that comes your way. Don't be a bottleneck. Pass relevant information onto appropriate people.*

**4** *If you can choose between reading a 50-page document or speaking to the author, speak to the author first, then read the document. You'll be in a better position to understand it quickly.*

**5** *Prioritize your reading.*

**6** *Plan your reading according to when you'll use the information and how complex it is (read technical information when you're fresh and alert).*

**7** *Don't be put off by other people's deadlines. Their deadline is their responsibility. Your stress levels are your responsibility.*

**8** *Take notes during meetings (even if you never read them again). It will keep you awake.*

**9** *Reduce your reading at work as much as possible by using the five-step system on everything.*

**10** *Never stop learning. There will always be something new.*

# 10

Working and studying for a living

In this chapter you will learn:
- *what taking a study course entails*
- *how to prepare for assessments and exams*
- *how to manage your time effectively*

If you are working and studying at the same time, it is important that what you want to achieve is achievable and consistent with your other commitments. It is easy to be so absorbed in the extra work that you forget the time you need to spend with your family and friends. If you work and study and don't give yourself enough quality recovery time (rest and play), your stress levels will increase and your effectiveness will decrease – thus defeating the entire object.

In this chapter we shall look at what taking a study course (e.g. an MBA or Open University course) entails and what you can do to make life easier, productive and successful when you are working and studying.

Advice is given on preparing for exams; this will be of value to those embarking on courses that use formal assessment methods. Although an increasing number of courses, especially modular ones, do not involve exams.

## Before you begin

Whether you are going into the first, second or third year of a course, there are some crucial things to think about before you begin.

### TIME AVAILABLE

Do you honestly have the time to do the course justice? Some of us will say 'No' but do the course anyway. If that applies to you, make sure that your reasons for doing the course are solid. Whatever those reasons are, make sure that you can put some time aside. Try to make study time at a set time of the day. Start putting that time aside for a month or so before you begin the course. This will give your family time to adjust to your new routine and will allow you to become used to spending that time studying. Sit quietly and focus your mind by doing some preparatory reading.

## If there is still a problem

If time is really a problem and you have to do the course, limit the amount of time you spend on each session. It is better to study for 30 minutes three or four times a week and several hours at the weekend than to spend no time at all in studying during the week and the whole day on Saturday or Sunday. Little and often is the recipe – like a healthy diet.

## ACCESS TO RESOURCES

Do you have access to all the resources you are going to need? Are you a member of the nearest library? Do you need to become a member of a university library? They often have texts that an ordinary library does not have. Do you know people you could speak to and discuss issues with? You may be able to make contact with appropriate lecturers at a local university. Do you have reliable access to the Internet?

## SUPPORT FROM FAMILY AND FRIENDS

Get your family involved. You need their support for two reasons:

1 *To give you the space and time to work.*
2 *To push you along when you are feeling a little demotivated (which will happen from time to time).*

If you have children, teach them to speed read and use pictures, books or ideas from your course (depending on their ages) to give them an awareness of what you are doing. Get your partner involved as well if he/she wants to be. When you get your timetable for the year ahead, put it on the fridge door so that everyone can see what you are committed to.

## DESIRE AND PURPOSE

Make sure you and your family know exactly why you are doing this course. What is the pay-off? Is it big enough to compensate for the weekend reading you will have to do?

## PRE-COURSE PREPARATION

There are several ways of preparing for the course:

▶ *During the month before you start, gather information that will help you during the course, revise notes from previous courses and read other related material.*

- You can also set up a good filing system for your assignments and reading materials.
- Build mind-maps or index cards of everything you already know.
- Every day, list at least five questions you want to answer through taking the course.
- On a daily basis, ask yourself why you are taking the course. If you keep saying, 'I don't know', then reassess whether you should go ahead or not.

## BREAKING DOWN A STUDY COURSE

The week you get your first course materials is very important. One of the mistakes people make is to read what they have to read only when they are told they should read it. To benefit fully from every piece of reading and work you do, follow these steps – they do work:

- Read your list of assignments first. If you can get hold of any past exam papers at this time in the course, do so.
- Once you have had a look at what assignments you have to deliver, follow the five-step system and go through the first four steps from prepare (which you have been doing in a general sense for the past few weeks) to active reading. Do this for all the books, articles and papers you have. As you read, take thorough notes of what you find interesting, what looks challenging, what seems to be familiar and what is totally new to you. Always keep in mind the assignments you will have to complete.
- Next, go through the list of questions you have built up over the month before the course, answer those you can and add more to the list if necessary.
- Study your timetable, determine what has to be studied by when and break down your reading into manageable chunks.

## Timetabling

When you design your timetable, don't make every day a study day. Try to keep two days a week free of coursework. These are for quality recovery time and for use if you miss one of your designated study days. It is also a good idea to be at least a week ahead of your course. There may be times when you miss several reading sessions in a row and catching up will put pressure on you and increase your stress levels. Take the time at the start of the course to plan, it will be the best time spent.

## Managing time

### PREPARING FOR MORE THAN ONE ASSIGNMENT AT A TIME

Although most assignments are on different subjects within your course, many of these subjects may be somehow related. When you are doing the research for one assignment, always keep in mind what the next one or two are about. You will be able to save a lot of time by doing this. If you come across an idea or section of text that would be useful for future assignments, write it down, add a note about why you thought it was a good idea or what made you notice it in the first place and include the title of the source and the page number. Then file it in the system you developed before the course began.

### PREPARING FOR THE EXAM FROM THE START OF THE COURSE

A mistake many people make is to put off any thought of studying for exams until they are almost at the end of the course. If you start preparing at the beginning of the course and keep exams in mind as you write and submit essays and projects, instead of panicking about the exam a week before you will have several weeks available for stress-free revision.

## Revising

The more revision you do as you go, the better your progress will be. When you begin to revise for an exam, few things are more alarming than the discovery that material seems unfamiliar to you even though you know you have already read it and perhaps even written an assignment on it.

Make it a habit to revise every day. At the start of each revision session spend 20 minutes going over past notes, mind-maps and index cards to refresh your memory. As you do this, link in different ideas and add new thoughts to your growing collection of knowledge. The more you can integrate your thinking, the more natural revision will become. If you revise a little every day all you need to do for the exam is to review your notes (much like you have every day since the start of the course) and add new thoughts or ideas to an already thorough body of knowledge – to make this easier, double space your notes so that you have the room to add comments later.

### Preparation for an exam if you have managed to structure your course

If you have managed to structure your course and if you have revised daily and begun to prepare for the exam at the start of the course instead of waiting until the end, you will be fully prepared and ready to sit a successful exam.

### Preparing for the exam if you have not structured your course

If you have not had time to structure your course or if you are halfway through a course already, there is a way to make sure you are able to sit the exam confidently. Here is a procedure to structure your reading so that you succeed without undue stress:

▶ *Determine how many study days you have before the exam or end of the course. Be realistic about this. If you are working full-time as well as studying, remember that you will have only early mornings, evenings and weekends and that you have to fit a life in there somewhere.*

- ▶ *Establish exactly what you have to study. Generally you will have a number of books and perhaps a few CDs, a few television programmes and notes from lectures. If you gather all the material together you will see that the amount of information you have to take in is finite. This will help your morale.*
- ▶ *Go through the course timetable and notes and make a list of all the different areas you have to cover.*
- ▶ *Under each heading write down the chapters, CDs, videos and lectures (all sources) you have to refer to for information.*
- ▶ *Organize the headings in an information order. Some areas of a subject serve as good background for others, so cover those first. The order in which you study these areas is entirely up to you and will depend on your current knowledge base.*
- ▶ *Once all areas are covered and you have identified the sources for each, put them in a sequence and create a realistic and achievable timetable. Do remember QRT (quality recovery time).*
- ▶ *The timetable you create should not have you starting at 4 a.m. and beginning again as soon as you get home – if you do that you will burn out. Make space in your timetable for plenty of QRT.*
- ▶ *Enjoy the learning process by rewarding yourself for each accomplishment (at least once a day). Choose ways that don't run up your dental bills or medical visits – try cycling, a walk in the countryside or a swim. Avoid chocolate or coffee if you can, but if coffee is what you want, take Dr Chris Fenn's advice (see Chapter 11) and make it the best.*

If you are studying and working at the same time the most important things to have are a clear objective, a clear purpose and as much support as you can muster. Most important of all, enjoy yourself and have fun!

# TEN THINGS TO REMEMBER

1 *Make the time in your day (everyday) to study little and often. It's better than cramming it all in at the last minute.*

2 *If you have a full-time job and a family and a social life, be honest about what you can do. Don't sacrifice sleep for study. It'll do damage in the long run.*

3 *At work, make lunch breaks study breaks. You'll be surprised how much you can achieve in half an hour.*

4 *Get support from your family and friends.*

5 *Use what you learn on the course as quickly as possible. The more practically useful it is, the more motivated you'll be to study.*

6 *Don't rely on course material alone. Expand your reading. You might not use the additional information to pass your exam but it will boost your knowledge and enjoyment of the subject.*

7 *Plan your work and stick to the plan! But be flexible. Modify your schedule if it doesn't work.*

8 *Know your assignments at the start of the course and angle your reading and research towards him.*

9 *Take days off! You need a life.*

10 *Get learning buddies and attend as many tutorials and summer schools as the course provides. Interaction with people going through the same issues might just save your sanity.*

# 11

Useful information and speed practice text

In this chapter you will learn:
- *prefix, suffix and root – the makings of a word*
- *critical language for critical reading*
- *how to establish your present reading rate*

## The makings of language

The following is information you might find useful. It is by no means a necessary prerequisite to beginning to practise speed reading. The more skills and information you have, however, the faster your reading will become. This information will be particularly useful if English is your second language.

### EXERCISE 1

This exercise is concerned with what is in a word:

▶ *Study the roots, suffixes and prefixes below.*
▶ *Think of your spoken, written and recognized vocabulary.*
▶ *Think of a word that comes from each prefix, suffix and root.*

**Roots**

| Roots | Meaning | Roots | Meaning |
|-------|---------|-------|---------|
| aer | air | mort | death |
| am | love | omni | all |
| ann | year | pat | father |
| aud | hear | path | suffering, feeling |
| bio | life | ped | foot |
| cap | take | photo | light |
| cap | head | phobe, phobia | fear |
| chron | time | pneum | air, breath, spirit |
| cor | heart | pos, posit | place |
| corp | body | poss, pot, poten | be able |
| de | god | quaerere | ask, question, seek |
| dic, dict | say, speak | rog | ask |
| duc | lead | scrib, scrip | write |
| ego | I | sence, sent | feel |
| equi | equal | sol | alone |
| fac, fic | make, do | soph | wise |
| frat | brother | spect | look |
| geo | earth | spir | breathe |
| graph | write | therm | warm |
| loc | place | ten | stretch, hold |
| loqu | speak | utilis | useful |
| luc | light | ven, vent | come, arrive |
| man | hand | vers, vert | turn |
| miss, mit | send | vid, vis | see |

## Prefixes

| Prefix | Meaning | Prefix | Meaning |
|--------|---------|--------|---------|
| a-, an- | without, not | equi- | equally |
| ab-, abs- | away, from, apart | extra- | outside, beyond |
| ad-, ac-, af- | to, towards | for-, fore- | before |
| aero- | air | hemi- | half |
| amb-, ambi- | both, around | hepta- | seven |
| amphi- | both, around | hexa- | six |
| ante- | before | homo- | same |
| anti- | against | hyper- | above, excessive |
| apo- | away from | il- | not |
| arch- | chief, most important | in-, im- | not |
| auto- | self | inter- | among, between |
| be- | about, make | intra-, intro- | inside, within |
| bene- | well, good | iso- | equal, same |
| bi- | two | mal- | bad, wrong |
| by, bye- | added to | meta- | after, beyond |
| cata- | down | mis- | wrongly |
| cente-, centi- | hundred | mono- | one, single |
| circum- | around | multi- | many |
| co-, col-, com-, cor- | together | non- | not |
| con- | with | ob-, oc-, of-, op- | in the way of, resistant to |
| contra- | against, counter | octa-, octo- | eight |
| de- | remove, down | off- | away, apart |
| deca-, deci- | ten | out- | beyond |
| demi- | half | over- | above |
| dia- | through, between | para- | aside, beyond |
| dis- | not, opposite to | penta- | five |
| duo- | two | per- | through |
| dys- | ill, hard | peri- | around, about |
| e-, ex- | out of | poly- | many |
| ec- | out of | post- | after |
| en-, in-, em-, im- | into, not | pre- | before |
| epi- | upon, at, in addition | prime-, primo- | first, important |
| | | pro- | in front of, favouring |

[Cont

| Prefix | Meaning | Prefix | Meaning |
|--------|---------|--------|---------|
| quadri- | four | ter- | three times |
| re- | again, back | tetra- | four |
| retro- | backward | trans- | across, through |
| se- | aside | tri- | three |
| self- | personalizing | ultra- | beyond |
| semi- | half | un- | not |
| sub- | under | under- | below |
| super- | above, over | uni- | one |
| syl- | with, together | vice- | in place of |
| syn-, sym- | together | yester- | preceding time |
| tele- | far, at or to a distance | | |

## Suffixes

| Suffixes | Meaning | Suffixes | Meaning |
|----------|---------|----------|---------|
| -able, -ible | capable of, fit for | -dom | condition or |
| -acy | state or quality of | -en | control small, |
| -age | action or state of | -er | quality belonging |
| -al, -ial | relating to | -ess | to feminine suffix |
| -an (ane, inan) | the nature of | -et, -ette | small |
| -ance, -ence | quality or action | -ferous | producing |
| -ant | of forming | -ful | full of |
| | adjectives | -fy, -ify | make |
| | of quality, | -hood | state or condition of |
| | nouns | -ia | names or classes, |
| | signifying a | | names of places, |
| | personal | -ian | practitioners or |
| | agent or | | inhabitants |
| | something | -ic | relating to |
| -arium, -orium | *see* -able, -ible | -id | a quality |
| | place for | -ine | a compound |
| -ary | place for, deal with | -ion | condition or |
| -ate | cause to be, office | | action of |
| -action | of action or state | -ish | a similarity or |
| -cle, -icle | of diminutive | | relationship |

| Suffixes | Meaning | Suffixes | Meaning |
|---|---|---|---|
| -ism | quality or doctrine of | -meter, -metry | of measurement |
| -ist | one who practises | -mony | resulting condition |
| -itis | inflammation of (medical) | -oid | resembling |
| | | -or | a state or action, a person or thing who |
| -ity, -ety, -ty | state or quality of | | |
| -ive | nature of | | |
| -ize, -ise | make, practise, act like | -ose, -ous | possessing, resembling |
| -lent | fullness | -osis | full of |
| -less | lacking | -some | process or condition of |
| -logy | indicating a branch of knowledge | -stable | producing an effect |
| -ly | having the quality of | -tude | like |
| | | -ward | quality or degree of |
| -ment | act or condition | -y | direction, condition |

## Critical language for critical reading

### EXERCISE 2

The following words are essential. Improve your use of them:

- ▶ *Write down a definition of each word.*
- ▶ *Look them up if you are not sure about them.*
- ▶ *Become familiar with them and enjoy thinking critically (but with an open mind).*

| Critical language | |
| --- | --- |
| Analysis | |
| Assumption | |
| Conclusion | |
| Connotation | |
| Denotation | |
| Evaluation | |
| Evidence | |
| Figurative language | |
| Generalization | |
| Interpretation | |
| Inference | |
| Judgement | |
| Metaphor | |
| Opinion | |
| Simile | |
| Symbol | |
| Tone | |
| Valid | |

## Establishing your current reading rate

The method for measuring your reading rate is explained in
Chapter 2 (p. 25). If you choose not to use a selection of books to
establish your reading rate, use the following piece of text from
*The Energy Advantage* by Dr Chris Fenn (printed with the author's
permission). The contents are also relevant and useful.

# The benefits of giving up caffeine

I found out, from personal experience, the benefits of giving up the stimulant and not relying on caffeine to get me through each day. It all began a few years ago when a friend of mine came to me for advice, complaining that he was lacking in energy. He had just started a new job in which he wanted to do well, but each morning he would drag his 38-year-old body out of bed and then struggle through the rest of the day. Each day he would dash to the station to catch the early train to work and then sleep for the whole two-hour journey, thinking that he was tired because of his early start. When he arrived at the office, he would immediately reach for the coffee jar before he could even begin to think about doing anything else. 'I needed a cup of coffee to get me started and then I drank tea and coffee throughout the day.' He also ate chocolate bars, hoping that they would give him the quick energy boost that he needed. No matter what he did, he always felt tired, and with crucial meetings and presentations to give, each day was a real struggle. He wanted me to give him some new energy pill or vitaminized drink that would boost his system.

Once I'd had a look at the details of what he was eating, I decided not to put something into his diet to boost his energy levels, but to take a couple of things out. One of these was sugar, the other was caffeine. I also realised that I was drinking a lot of coffee so, four years ago, we both agreed to give up caffeine. It proved to be a challenge for us both, especially getting through the initial withdrawal symptoms. We suffered severe headaches, tension at the back of the neck and bad temper – it all felt rather like a dose of flu and lasted for about five days. But, oh was it worth it; we are now changed people! My friend no longer feels tired and has to buy two quality newspapers which he reads from cover to cover on the journey to work. He doesn't touch the coffee jar and no longer craves chocolate.

(Contd)

He feels alive, really enjoys his work and is much more productive because he feels so well – even though he is still under a lot of pressure. I, too, feel different and much less tense without caffeine flooding my system every day. I have even more energy than I used to (which for a nutritionist is a good advert!) and I am calmer, even though I run my own consultancy business, write books and articles for magazines and newspapers, give seminars and lectures, design and run my own courses and do television and radio work! I enjoy the flavour of coffee, but if I drink it now I soon feel sluggish and develop a headache. I prefer to relish the aroma when I visit a coffee house, which is much more pleasant than the effects caffeine has on my system.

Although I was overjoyed at the benefits that two people found when they gave up caffeine, it got me thinking – I wonder if other people experience the same benefits. Plenty of studies have been done to examine the effects of caffeine on blood pressure or heart rate or kidney function, but not one, as far as I was aware, had investigated the effects on personality and general mental performance. I had a contract with the Lifestyle Health Promotion programme which was run for the giant oil exploration and production company, Shell Expro UK. This involved travelling to a number of production platforms in the North Sea to give talks and seminars to the offshore teams. Alcohol is banned offshore – but an awful lot of coffee and other sources of caffeine are consumed instead. Here was an ideal opportunity to carry out a small research project on the effects of giving up (or cutting down) caffeine. It was a very simple study and involved filling in questionnaires. First, volunteers were asked questions relating to who they were, their work schedule, how much caffeine they consumed each day, and to give a self-assessed rating of their physical and mental state. They then agreed to take the 'Caffeine Challenge', which was to give up caffeine for a month. At the end of the four weeks, they were sent a second questionnaire, again asking them to rate and describe their mood and mental state. As the questionnaires came flooding in, it was clear that individuals working offshore certainly did consume a large amount of caffeine (the average daily intake was 929 mg). Office workers based on-shore were also encouraged to take the 'Caffeine Challenge' and, with a coffee machine on every floor, they too heavily relied on the stimulant (average daily intake was 903 mg). A dose of 100 mg (the amount usually found in a single cup of coffee) will normally produce the stimulating effects we associate with the drug. An intake over 500 mg per day is considered high, and is the level at which many individuals begin to experience the downside of the stimulant's effects: moodiness, anxiety, restlessness and tension.

I was amazed and surprised at the number of ways many of the 'guinea pigs' had benefited from cutting out caffeine or significantly reducing their intake. Several offshore engineers reported that they no longer had headaches and could work much more productively as a team because they were no longer so tense and wound up. The safety officer was delighted when his tinnitus (buzzing, thumping, ringing sound in the ears) was cured. Mike, working in the helicopter flight control room, announced that he had tried to give up smoking every year for the past 16 years, but always caved in after a couple of weeks. Since giving up caffeine, he has gone for seven months without a cigarette. 'I always associated smoking with drinking coffee, but now I don't miss either!'

Paul worked as a computer programmer, which he enjoyed, but every weekend he suffered from headaches and felt generally depressed, tired and anxious. His wife objected to his grumpy moods, especially as they soon disappeared once he was back at work and away from her! Taking part in the 'Caffeine Challenge' highlighted the fact that he drank strong coffee continually throughout the day, which meant at weekends, when he hardly drank any, he was displaying withdrawal symptoms. Paul reckoned that changing his coffee drinking habits at work probably saved his marriage! I no doubt eased his overworked kidneys too. Caffeine is a

*(Contd)*

diuretic, artificially stimulating the production of urine. Many of the 'Challenge' guinea pigs reported not having to visit the toilet so often (especially during the night), having cut down their caffeine intake! This has its own practical advantages, but it also means that the body retains more of the vital vitamins that are otherwise excreted with the increased flow of urine every day. Normally the kidneys are able to selectively excrete the toxic chemicals but retain other essential nutrients. In particular the B vitamins are lost when a lot of caffeine is taken. They play a crucial role in energy metabolism and so, with a high caffeine intake, the body is losing the very nutrients that are not only in the mind, but also the body!

## CAFFEINE AND SLEEP

The highly subjective reports from individuals who noticed that they slept much more soundly after taking part in the 'Caffeine Challenge' confirm the results of a much more controlled experiment, on the effects of caffeine on sleep, carried out in Japan. Volunteers who took 150 mg of caffeine then took an average of 126 minutes to get to sleep, compared with 29 minutes for those who had not taken caffeine. The caffeine users slept for a total of 281 minutes in the laboratory compared with 444 minutes for the non-caffeine users. Recordings of the electrical activity of the brain showed that caffeine in all cases significantly altered normal sleep patterns, and many other similar studies have confirmed these findings. They also show that caffeine users are more easily aroused by sudden noises, they move about and are generally a lot less settled during sleep – and on waking report that they don't feel as though they have had a good night's sleep.

The sleeping body gives the impression of being totally switched off; it is not. ... [Sleep] is a time when transmitters and cells are recharged, the brain recovers from the stresses and strains of the day, and tissues are revitalised. Overall, it is as vital for subconscious activity as for physical passivity.

There are two types of sleep: dream sleep, also known as REM (Rapid Eye Movement); and deep sleep, or non-REM. Any growth or repair of the body occurs during deep sleep, but REM (which occurs towards the end of the sleep time) is for psychological repair. This is the time when the mind can unwind, and sort through information stacked away in our sub-conscious during the day.

This is the best time for coming up with solutions to challenges that you simply couldn't figure out during waking hours. With inadequate REM sleep we become fretful, irritable, tense and less able to concentrate. It is thought that caffeine may affect the quality of REM sleep, and so contribute to feelings of restlessness at a deeper level.

By now you should be convinced that giving up (or cutting down) on your caffeine intake is worth a try. At the very least, you can only discover the benefits. A question I am often asked is: 'What do I drink instead?' Remember, it is important to drink at least three litres of fluid each day. When you give up coffee, you need to find a replacement beverage – which doesn't contain coffee – some colas and soft drinks contain caffeine and this is usually added as a flavouring and may be listed in the ingredients. ...

The exact amount of caffeine in a cup of coffee or tea varies tremendously. The range for coffee is 30–180 mg and for tea it is 20–60 mg. The wide variation is mainly because of the cup, the quantity and quality of the coffee or tea leaf used and the method of brew. For example, filter coffee surprisingly contains more caffeine than percolated coffee which in turn contains more than instant. This is because in making filter coffee, although the water passes over the beans only once, nearly all of the caffeine is dissolved out of the more finely ground coffee. Repeatedly washing the coffee, as in the percolated method, only causes more of the other substances in the bean to go into solution. Although the actual content of caffeine in tea is greater

(Contd)

than in coffee, on average a cup of tea usually contains less. Caffeine is also released from tea leaves more slowly, especially if the leaves are in tea bags.

It is possible to cut down your caffeine intake quite dramatically simply by drinking tea instead of coffee. This is good news for everyone who really enjoys a good cup of tea, or who has to choose a drink when only tea or coffee are on offer. Green China tea is virtually caffeine free and is best drunk without milk. It has an unusual smokey flavour and is perhaps an acquired taste. So are many of the new herb and fruit teas which are streaming onto the market as alternative caffeine-free drinks. In the past few years, sales of these in the UK have rocketed, and in 1996, we drank 1,397 million cups of herbal teas alone. This is small brew compared with other European countries; 70 per cent of Germans and 50 per cent of French people drink herbal teas daily. Herb teas are made with flowers, leaves and stems of all kinds of aromatic plants. Apart from being caffeine-free, their mild healing properties have been valued for centuries. If you want to experiment, try the following:

Camomile – to calm your digestion and as a gentle sedative and relaxant.
Peppermint – to aid digestion and relieve flatulence.
Nettle – as a general tonic, but also to settle nerves.
Lime flowers – to relieve anxiety and nervous tension.
Ginger – an internal antiseptic and anti-inflammatory agent.
Elderflower – a general tonic and mild laxative.

Fruit teas are simply flavoured water. If you read the list of ingredients you will find that any fruit tea will always include hibiscus and rose hip. These give what the tea manufacturers call 'body'. Flavourings are then added to the basic mix to create anything from strawberry tea to more exotic blends such as 'Mango and Apple' or 'Passion fruit and Pear'. They are a good choice if you want a no-caffeine drink, and with all the varieties on the market, you won't get bored with the same flavour.

Coffee substitutes, which have never seen a coffee bean, are also available and popular on the Continent. They usually contain a mixture of roasted barley, chicory, figs, rye, wheat, dandelion root or acorns. Make sure you avoid the ones that contain guarana – a Brazilian herb and a source of caffeine!

### WHAT ABOUT DECAFFEINATED TEA AND COFFEE?

If you want to cut down on your caffeine intake, but still enjoy the flavour of coffee, then choose de-caff. Make sure that you check the label first because there are two methods used to decaffeinate the coffee beans; one is much healthier than the other.

Caffeine is removed from the coffee beans or tea leaves at the green stage, before roasting or fermentation, by 'washing' with water or a solvent. The solvent is either methyl chloride (the basis of paint stripper), or ethyl chloride (better known as a dry cleaning fluid!). These solvents can leave residues which are possibly as harmful as the caffeine they are removing. The other method, known as the Swiss Water Method, involves water, carbon dioxide and steam to remove the caffeine. It is more expensive but obviously does not create harmful residues. Both methods involve heat treatments which can destroy some of the coffee flavour components.

Most decaffeinated tea is made using the solvent extraction method, but you need to read the label to check which method has been used. If the label is vague about the method of decaffeination, it has probably been done using the solvent method!

The pure caffeine that is extracted is not wasted. It is ladled back into soft drinks and also many over-the-counter cold remedies and headache pills. So, if you suffer from a withdrawal headache as you cut down on your caffeine intake, remember not to reach for an alternative source in the form of a headache pill!

## QUESTIONS

1 What did the author's friend want from the author?
   What did he get instead?
2 What two substances did the author recommend her friend
   cut out?
3 The author joined in the exercise. True or false?
4 What symptoms did they suffer from as a result of cutting
   those substances out?
5 What effect of caffeine did the author focus on for a study
   and which company did she approach?
6 How long did the volunteers have to give up caffeine?
   For 3 weeks/1 month/2 months?
7 What were the results from the experiments regarding the
   effects of caffeine on sleep?
8 What are the two types of sleep?
9 What happens during each one?
10 Is it important to drink 2, 3, or 4 litres of fluid per day?
11 What is the difference between herb teas and fruit teas?
12 What are some examples of coffee substitutes?
13 What is guarana?
14 Describe the two different ways of decaffeinating coffee.
15 Where does the caffeine extracted from coffee go?

# TEN THINGS TO REMEMBER

1 *Understand the language you speak.*

2 *Explore language patterns and structures.*

3 *Keep notes of the words you repeatedly trip over. Use them until you're comfortable with them.*

4 *Read conclusions and summaries first.*

5 *Be aware of the pace at which you read. If you get bored and your mind wanders, increase your reading rate.*

6 *Reduce your caffeine intake.*

7 *Get plenty of sleep.*

8 *If you get headaches when you read, get your eyes tested (and drink plenty of water).*

9 *Have fun with language.*

10 *Actually, just have fun, period.*

# 12

......................................................................................

# What next?

In this chapter you will:
* *receive advice on learning and developing new methods of reading*
* *learn how to turn them into habits*

## Guidelines for your 21-day programme

When you learn something new you are likely to go through a phase when you know that you know, but are aware that you haven't fully assimilated the new information yet. This is a most fragile time in learning. If you don't follow through and integrate what you have learned into your way of thinking and working, your efforts will be wasted. Receiving the information is easy – you read a book, go to a course, listen to a CD. When the information is in your head, what happens next is up to you: Do you use the information or not? Do you put your course books on the shelf until 'later' or not? Do you think 'Hmmm, interesting' and go back to your old habits?

Decision and action are needed. The decision takes a split second. Are you going to become the best you can be?

When you make such a decision, it is important to build a plan. The problem when you try to change habits is that old habits fight back. One way of making the change process easy is to create a daily plan. Instead of doing everything in one day and being overwhelmed, complete the task a bit at a time.

The rules for the 21-day programme are generally common sense:

▶ **Make your programme not too easy, not too difficult** – *The programme you create must be easy enough for you to know it is achievable and challenging enough to excite you.*

▶ **Select topics that interest you** – *If you have to read material that isn't particularly interesting during your normal working day, then choose other, more interesting material to develop your speed reading skills.*

▶ **Build in variety** – *One day, practise speed reading with a novel; the next day, try a newspaper; after that a magazine you've being wanting to read for a while. Each time the aim is to read as much as possible, using the most effective technique.*

▶ **Put aside 20 minutes each day** – *To practise speed reading, 20 minutes is a guideline. If you have only 10 minutes, that is fine as long as every day you spend that amount of time working on your new skill. There are exercises in Chapter 3 to help you. The best time to do your practice is in the morning because it will act as a reminder to you to pay attention to your reading as the day goes on. If you can only put 20 minutes aside in the evening, then remind yourself when you plan your day in the morning that you have put that time aside and that you intend to be aware of what you are reading throughout the day.*

▶ **Integrate your new knowledge** – *Use your skills during the day. Practise speed reading every time you read something: your mail, letters, newspapers, books, e-mails, memos, backs of cereal boxes – anything.*

▶ **Keep your purpose clear** – *If you do not have a purpose you will quickly lose interest. Keep in mind why you are learning how to read fast. What else do you want to do with the extra time you have? What will speed reading do for you?*

▶ **Practise daily** – *The more consistent your practice, the better you will become. If you speed read one day and forget for the* next few, the chances are that the number of days between practising will become more and more.

▶ **Teach someone else** – *When you can teach someone else what you have learnt, you have learnt it well. If you have children, teach them – any age is a good time for them to learn. If you can't answer all their questions use the five-step system to find the answers.*

▶ **Read in groups** – *Developing a reading group is an excellent way to ensure you practise. Meet once a month or more often if you like. Make the purpose of the group twofold: firstly, discuss the contents of the book, articles or papers you read; and, secondly, discuss the reading methods you used or had trouble with. Also, begin to explore other ways of reading effectively and bring those to the group. Group motivation will drive your learning forward. The more people you involve in your learning, the easier it will be to stay motivated. It helps when there is someone there to encourage you when you are having difficulties.*

▶ **Learn something new every day** – *No matter how small it is, add something new to your knowledge. Keep a notebook with you to record your daily mini-lesson. You will be surprised how fast your general knowledge grows.*

▶ **Learn a new word every day** – *The better your vocabulary is, the faster you will be able to read.*

▶ **Be flexible** – *If you find your programme is too easy or too difficult, change it.*

▶ **Don't stop after 21 days** – *After your first 21 days you will have integrated the basics of speed reading successfully, provided you have had sufficient practice. After that, take your reading to another level. You have already developed the habit of putting aside time to practise a new skill. Keep that time available and use it for developing another skill by applying your speed reading skills and extending them as you learn something else.*

▶ *A useful tip is to keep a small notebook in which to write down comments on the day's reading activities. You could use the one you keep to record each day's mini-lesson or a separate one. What did you feel or think as you read? What was easy? What was difficult? What would you change about the way you read that day? What questions do you have?*

## TIMETABLE TO HELP YOU DESIGN YOUR 21-DAY PROGRAMME

### Example

| Day | Reading material | Time | What did I learn? | New word |
|---|---|---|---|---|
| 1 | The morning paper in less than 20 minutes. Purpose: practise 5 steps and inform. | 20 min. (6.00–6.20) | New developments in the treatment of anaemia. | haemoglobin: protein that gives red blood cells their colour. |

| Day | Reading material | Time | What did I learn? | New word |
|---|---|---|---|---|
| 1 | | | | |
| 2 | | | | |
| 3 | | | | |
| 4 | | | | |
| 5 | | | | |
| 6 | | | | |
| 7 | | | | |
| 8 | | | | |
| 9 | | | | |
| 10 | | | | |
| 11 | | | | |
| 12 | | | | |
| 13 | | | | |
| 14 | | | | |
| 15 | | | | |
| 16 | | | | |
| 17 | | | | |
| 10 | | | | |
| 19 | | | | |
| 20 | | | | |
| 21 | | | | |

## Teach someone else the basics of speed reading

You may have a child, a friend or a partner who wants to learn. Here are some steps to follow to teach them effectively and, at the same time, consolidate your learning:

1 *Finish reading this book. Be sure to read the whole book and check that you fully understand it. If you are going to teach someone else, you must know what you are talking about. Have the book handy while you teach so that you can find answers to any questions that you might not be sure about. When you look up the answers, look them up together. That will involve both of you and will make the learning more of an active process for your student.*
2 *First, find out what your student already knows or thinks about speed reading and also what questions they have. Talk about their learning strategy.*
3 *Explain in a way that interests them (which may be different from what you would choose) a little about each aspect of speed reading that you are going to teach them. The following headings cover what a person needs to know to understand the basics:*
   ▷ *Determine their current reading rate.*
   ▷ *How to use a pacer to increase their reading rate.*
   ▷ *Different memory techniques.*
   ▷ *The five-step system.*
   ▷ *Effective use of eyes, including eye exercises.*
   ▷ *Flexible reading – reading different types of material.*
   ▷ *Problems and solutions.*

### DETERMINING YOUR STUDENT'S CURRENT READING RATE AND INCREASING IT

1 *To determine the reading rate see Chapter 2 (p. 25). Either use the text by Dr Chris Fenn in Chapter 11 (pp. 169–176) or get your student to select six different pieces of text. Draw up a speed reading graph for their use (see p. 40).*

2 *Once you have determined their reading rate, talk about the different factors that may inhibit speed reading and what they can do to eliminate them.*

3 *Explain how to use a pacer. Ask them to place a pen or finger at the start of each line and to keep up with your counting. Count from 1 to 10 five times, starting at approximately one count every 2 seconds and increasing it to two counts per second. Ask your student to keep up with you, no matter how fast you go, at a rate of one line per count. Tell them that if the pace is getting so fast that they cannot read each word, that is all right – all they are doing is getting used to using a pacer.*

4 *Once they are comfortable using a pacer, invite them to try some of the exercises outlined in Chapter 2.*

5 *Then give them a new text to read. Ask them to read as fast as they can for good comprehension, using a pacer.*

6 *Plot their speed on the graph. It will have increased.*

7 *Now, both of you take a break and have a cup of caffeine-free tea or coffee.*

## DIFFERENT MEMORY TECHNIQUES

1 *Once you have taken a break, ask your student to try to remember as much as they can from the texts just read.*

2 *Then find out what strategy they used. Did they just remember it? Did they write anything down? Did they already know something about the subject, so they found it easy to recall?*

3 *Next, to expand your student's skills go through each of the memory strategies outlined in Chapter 5 (pp. 79–90). Allow your student to experience them all.*

4 *When they have done that, put this book and any notes aside and get your student to tell you what they just read in as much detail as possible. Sometimes we think we understand and remember what we read, but if we have to tell someone else about it we find we cannot. If your student can tell you about the passage in sufficient detail, then the technique worked. You just have to determine whether it allowed them to read as fast as they wanted to.*

**5** *Remind your student that the best memory techniques are those that allow them to remember what they want to remember when they are reading as fast as they want to read.*

**6** *Also, when they select a memory technique they must think about when they are going to need to use the information again; this will determine what method they choose.*

## THE FIVE-STEP SYSTEM

**1** *Using the summaries of the five-step system (pp. xv–xvii and pp. 1–20), demonstrate to your student exactly how to use it. Do this with two different newspapers. Each of you takes one and goes through the five-step system. The aim of the process should be to gather as much general news as you can and to find the one story that interests you most.*

**2** *Once you have selected a story, use the memory technique each of you thinks suits the story best. Then, in turn, tell each other in as much detail as possible what the story was about.*

**3** *Time yourselves. Try to get through an entire newspaper in less than 15 minutes.*

## USING THEIR EYES EFFECTIVELY

You can both take part in this.

**1** *Supply your student with a copy of this book. Both of you do all the eye exercises in Chapter 8.*

**2** *At the end of each one, discuss what you noticed.*

**3** *Before you carry on, do another speed reading assessment.*

## FLEXIBLE READING

**1** *Gather together a collection of very different reading materials: letters, reports, book, articles, magazines, newspapers.*

**2** *Work with your student to read each one as fast as possible. Determine what the best approach for each one is as you go. Remember to state your purpose for reading the document.*

### PROBLEMS AND SOLUTIONS

1 *Spend some time talking about the different environments in which each of you reads, and what the different challenges associated with each are. Work out ways to get round them.*

2 *Finally, to test your long-term memory, both of you should recall as much as you can without referring to the texts you have read during this training.*

## Summary of the five-step system of effective reading

At the end of each step ask yourself:
What is my purpose? Do I have my answers yet?
Do I need to go further?

**Step 1**
What do I already know?
What do I still need to know?

**Step 2**
Overview of the book.
Eliminate unnecessary material and highlight areas that warrant further study.

**Step 3**
Familiarize yourself with the level of vocabulary (technical/layman).
Continue to highlight areas of interest.

**Step 4**
Read the first paragraph of each chapter and the first sentence of each paragraph.
Continue to eliminate unnecessary areas.

**Step 5**
Select what you need or want to read and then read it.

## The A to Z of effective reading

**A Active reading** Take notes, write in margins, circle, highlight, underline, think, argue, debate your way through whatever you read.

**B Believe** You are capable of phenomenal things. Make what you learn in this book your first step to effective reading. Look constantly for a better way of doing what you do. See the book list that follows for advice about where to go to reach the next level.

**C Comfort** Make sure your environment is as comfortable as possible. If it is not, then change it or move. If you can do neither, use multi-sensory reading to help maintain your attention and concentration and take a break every 15 minutes.

**Concentration** Practise concentration techniques. Remember that without concentration there is no memory, whether you are reading or whether you are taking in names.

**D Determination** Don't give up. Sometimes you might feel frustrated. This is a natural part of the learning process. In between your old habit and your new improved skill there may be a period when you know what you are capable of but also know that you haven't got it quite right yet. Learn to enjoy this feeling; it means you are going in the right direction. Take the time to sit back, re-affirm your purpose, relax and carry on.

**E Enjoy** The more you enjoy reading, the less stressed you will be and the better you will remember what you read. When you state your purpose include enjoyment as part of it.

**F Five-step system** Apply it to everything you read.

**Flexibility** Remember that you don't have to read fast all the time. Develop the skill of being able to identify when you can read fast and when you have to slow down.

**G Groups** Work with other people. Sometimes a group of brains is better at staying motivated than one working alone.

**H Harassed** If you are feeling stressed or tired your effectiveness will diminish. Stop and take a break, especially if you feel you do not have the time to do that.

**I Ideas** Cross-reference, combine and elaborate on ideas between texts. Play the 'What if' game with new ideas. Ask what would happen if X happened instead of Y. What would happen if you can read a page a second?

**J Justify** Make sure you justify doing each piece of reading someone else asks you to do. Always ask yourself why you have to read it and what call it will have on your time.

**K Knowledge** Make increasing your knowledge of yourself and the world around you a daily goal.

**L Learn** Make it a habit to learn something new from your reading every day.

**M Manageable chunks** Avoid reading for more than 30 minutes at a time. Break up your reading into chunks that can be achieved in that period of time. If you have a lot of reading to do, set a clock to remind you to take a break.

**Memory** Improve it by breaking your reading up as advised.

**N Novels** Using the five-step system for novels may spoil the ending. You will find, however, that the speed at which you can read novels will increase as a result of your speed reading practice. You will not lose any of the enjoyment; in fact, you may find you finish more of the novels that you begin.

**O Organized** Clear your desk of everything other than what you are working on at the time. Create a good filing system of ideas, books, papers and references. Organize your learning. Decide what you want to learn, where you are going to find it and how you are going to set about doing so.

**P Pacer** Use a pacer to increase your speed whenever you are reading, especially when you are tired.

**Purpose** Have a clear and definite purpose whenever you read anything.

**Q Question** Always ask questions. Just because what the author has said is in print, that does not mean that they are right.

**R Revise** Refer to notes you have made previously whenever you have the opportunity to do so. Sometimes we only appreciate something later. Also, revision is vital for recall.

**S Stretch** Your body is involved in your reading as well as your mind. Reading can be a passive activity. When you read for any length of time your body may become stiff. Stretch your body whenever you take a break. If you feel that you are losing concentration make a good stretch the first thing you do.

**T Time** Take time to develop any new skill. Enjoy the gap between knowing you don't know how to do something and achieving success. Be patient with yourself.

**U Use** The more you use the information you learn, the better you will remember it and be able to apply it when you need it. Teach someone else, write a report, an article or a book, discuss what you read with others.

**V** **Vocabulary** Use Steps 2 and 3 (preview and passive reading) to identify words you don't understand. Look them up before you continue. If you encounter a word you don't understand while you are reading, take note, keep going and look it up at the end of the paragraph or section. You may find that the meaning becomes clear in the context of the text.

**W** **Work is play with a suit on** Make whatever you do fun and you will be able to carry on longer and perform more effectively.

**X** **Explore** Find information from as many different sources as possible. Sometimes you can get what you are looking for in a text more quickly from a phone call to an expert or a friend.

**Y** **You** Reading and learning is a personal skill. Often you are the only one involved when you have to perform. Make sure that the techniques you use work for you. Try a variety of different ways of reading and learning and create a set of tools that suits you.

**Z** **ZZZ** Sleep. Avoid reading and studying at the expense of a good night's sleep. Take breaks whenever you need them.

# TEN THINGS TO REMEMBER

1 *Design a 21-day programme to help you develop your reading habits further.*

2 *Do something different. If you put this book down and go back to your old habits you will have wasted your time and will continue to do so by reading ineffectively.*

3 *Practise on everything from cornflakes boxes to encyclopaedias.*

4 *Talk about what you read.*

5 *Learn something new every day.*

6 *Be interested in what you're reading – even if you have to con yourself into it.*

7 *Read what you're interested in.*

8 *Have a clear purpose.*

9 *In case you missed the last top tip have a clear purpose, regardless of what you're reading.*

10 *One more time (just because your memory might need some help): know why you're reading something.*

# Taking it further

These are only a few of the resources available to you to continue your development. In some cases, the entire book is excellent; others will have gems that are worth looking for. Look for new information everywhere. Attend as many courses as you can. Remember that not everything has to be read – learn from audio programmes.

www.madaboutbooks.com: Quality information from Hodder and Stoughton

www.chrisfenn.com: For more information on Dr Chris Fenn. To obtain Dr Chris Fenn's book, *The Energy Advantage*, contact the author at Input Nutrition, 19 Craigton Court, Aberdeen, Scotland AB15 7PF

Beaver, Diana, *Lazy Learning*, Element, 1994

Berg and Conyers, *Speed Reading the Easy Way*, Barron's, 1998

Berg, Howard S., *Super Reading Secrets*, Warner Books, 1992

Buzan, Tony, *The Speed Reading Book*, BBC, 1997

Cutler, Wade E., *Triple Your Reading Speed*, Macmillan, 1993

Coman and Heavers, *What You Need to Know About Reading Comprehension and Speed, Skimming and Scanning, Reading for Pleasure*, National Textbook Company, 1995, 1998

Davis, Eshelman, McKay, *The Relaxation and Stress Reduction Handbook*, New Harbinger Publications, 1998

DePorter, Bobbi and Hernacki, Mike, *Quantum Learning*, Piatkus, 1995

Dryden, Gordon and Vos, Jeannette, *The Learning Revolution*, Accelerated Learning, 1994

Dudley, Geoffrey A., *Rapid Reading*, Thorsons, 1997

Dudley, Geoffrey A., *Double your Learning Power*, Thorsons, 1986

Fenn, Chris, *The Energy Advantage*, Thorsons, 1997

Fritz, George, *The Open Focus Handbook*, Biofeedback Computers, 1982

Herrmann, J., Raybeck, J., and Gutman, J., *Improving Student Memory*, Hogrefe and Huber Publishers, 1996

Hooper, Judith and Teresi, Dick, *The Three Pound Universe*, Tarcher Putnam, 1992

Hunt, D.T., *Learning to Learn*, Elan, 1993

King, Graham, *The Secrets of Speed Reading*, Mandarin, 1994

Khalsa, Dharma Singh, Dr, *Brain Longevity*, Century, 1997

Konstant, Tina, *Successful Speed Reading in a Week*, Hodder and Stoughton, 2001

Konstant, Tina and Taylor, Morris, *Mental Space*, Pearson Education, 2002

Konstant, Tina and Taylor, Morris, *Managing Information Overload*, Hodder Education, 2008

Leo Angart (Presented by), *Vision: The Minds Eye*, NLP Asia Ltd

Lorayne, Harry, *Improve Exam Results in 30 Days*, Thorsons, 1992

Luria, A.R., *The Mind of a Mnemonist*, Harvard, 1968

McKim, Robert H., *Experiences in Visual Thinking*, PWS Publishing

Northledge, *The Good Study Guide*, The Open University, 1990

Ostrander, S. and Schroeder, L., *Superlearning 2000*, Souvenir Press, 1994

Ostrander, S. and Schroeder, L., *Cosmic Memory*, Simon and Schuster, 1992

Rose, Colin, *Accelerated Learning*, Accelerated Learning Systems Ltd, 1995

Rozakis, Laurie E., *21st Century Guide to Increasing your Reading Speed*, 21st Century Works, 1996

Rozakis, Laurie, *Power Reading*, Macmillan

Schwartz, David J., *Maximise Your Mental Power*, Thorsons, 1986

Szantesson, Ingemar, *Mind Mapping and Memory*, Kogan Page, 1994

Treacy, Declan, *Clear Your Desk*, Arrow, 1998

Turley, Joyce, *Speed Reading in Business*, Crisp Publications, 1989

Wenick, Lillian P., *Speed Reading Naturally*, Prentice Hall International, 1990

# Index